Vintage Virginia

✦ A History of Good Taste ✦

© P. Buckley Moss, 1998

The Virginia Dietetic Association Cookbook

Vintage Virginia
A History of Good Taste

Copyright © 2000
Virginia Dietetic Association
P.O. Box 439, Centreville, Virginia 20122 • 703-815-8293
www.eatright-va.org

Library of Congress Number: 00-131181
ISBN: 0-9673874-0-X

Designed, Edited, and Manufactured by
Favorite Recipes® Press
an imprint of

FRP

P.O. Box 305142, Nashville, Tennessee 37230
800-358-0560

Managing Editor: Mary Cummings
Project Manager: Debbie Van Mol, RD
Art Director: Steve Newman
Book Design: Jim Scott
Project Production: Sara Anglin

Manufactured in the United States of America
First Printing: 2000   10,000 copies

Bed and Breakfast and restaurant recipes reprinted from *Favorite Breakfast & Brunch Recipes II*
with permission of the Virginia Department of Agriculture and Consumer Services.

Artwork reproduced with the permission of P. Buckley Moss from the
archives of the P. Buckley Moss Museum, Waynesboro, Virginia.

TABLE OF CONTENTS

INTRODUCTION

Virginia is for lovers of good taste . . . past and present. The Virginia Dietetic Association takes great pride in compiling *Vintage Virginia*—a unique collage of historical facts, cooking and nutrition tips, and delicious recipes from across time and the regions of our Commonwealth. For nearly 400 years, since our ancestors settled Jamestown in 1607, Virginians have enjoyed a history of good taste. Many of the classics herein are derived from the kitchens of our great-grandmothers and reflect our rich southern heritage, while others are contemporary treasures from members' private collections including quick and easy recipes.

Each of the recipes contained in *Vintage Virginia* has been selected and tested by Virginia's nutrition experts. We number more that 1500 Registered Dietitians and Technicians who are members of the Virginia Affiliate of the American Dietetic Association—"Your Link to Nutrition and Health."[SM] Our mission to "serve the public through the promotion of optimal nutrition, health and well being" is reflected in these pages. It is our belief that ALL FOODS FIT in a healthy diet and should be enjoyed in moderation. We support the marriage of good taste and nutrition to promote lifelong eating habits that bring both pleasure and wellness to our tables and lives.

Profits from the sale of this cookbook will sustain our mission and profession in our continuing efforts to keep pace with the evolving science of nutrition in the new millennium. Thanks for your support. We sincerely hope that you will enjoy *Vintage Virginia* as much as we have in bringing it to fruition.

To your health and pleasure!

ACKNOWLEDGEMENTS

Cookbook Steering Committee

Chairman

    Ann A. Hertzler, Ph.D., R.D., C.F.C.S.

Marketing

    Lucy Garman, M.S., R.D.
    Jennifer Tu, R.D.

Recipe Selection

    Peggy Morgan, R.D.
    Cindy Shufflebarger, R.D.

Recipe Testing

    Janet W. Gloeckner, Ph.D., R.D., C.F.C.S.

Sidebar Production

    Jane W. Blosser, M.S., R.D.
    Jean Robbins, Ph.D., Retired R.D.
    Ann A. Hertzler, Ph.D., R.D., C.F.C.S.

Design

    Rita P. Smith, M.S., R.D.

Administrative Support

    Jackie Darling, R.D.

At Large

    Mindy Facenda, R.D.
    Carol Jones, R.D.
    Beverly Kates, M.S., R.D.
    Kathleen Walters, M.S., R.D.

ABOUT THE ARTIST

P. Buckley Moss
"The People's Artist"

Pat Buckley Moss was born on May 20, 1933, in New York City. When it was determined that Pat, at a young age, was artistically gifted, she attended the Washington Irving High School for the Fine Arts in Manhattan, where her talents were seriously nourished. In 1951 Pat received a scholarship to New York's Cooper Union for the Advancement of Science and Art. She studied at this prestigious art school for four years and specialized in fine arts and graphic design. Soon after leaving school she married, had six children, and eventually settled in Waynesboro in the Shenandoah Valley of Virginia. It was here that Pat came to appreciate the quiet beauty of rural scenery and to know the picturesque and deeply religious Amish and Mennonite people. Soon she was incorporating these elements into her art, creating an impetus that revitalized her artistic career and reignited her ambitions. Today, thousands of collectors throughout the world have come to appreciate and treasure Pat's art with its distinctive look and its great popular appeal. She has received numerous honors, awards, and recognitions for her work. Although Pat Moss now enjoys tremendous artistic success, she has become equally well-known for her dedicated work with special education groups and her generous donations to children-related charities.

Virginia Landscape

© P. Buckley Moss, 1998

BEGINNING AT JAMESTOWN

An Old Receipt for Blackberry Cordial

To two Quarts Blackberry Juice add one Pound Loaf sugar, four grated nutmegs, one-quarter ounce ground cloves, one-quarter ounce ground allspice, one-quarter ounce ground cinnamon. Simmer all together, for thirty Minutes, in a stew pan closely covered. Strain through a Cloth when cold and add a pint of the best French Brandy.

The Williamsburg Art of Cookery
Mrs. Helen Bullock

"Heaven and Earth Never Agreed Better To Frame A Place for Man's Habitation". Thus spoke Captain John Smith about Virginia and true it was, but first the settlers had to adjust to their new environment—an adjustment that was costly. For two years after their settlement in 1607, there was inadequate food production. The colonists were forced to subsist mainly on corn and wildlife as Captain Smith could obtain from the Indians.

Interesting Facts About Virginia Foods, 1607–1700

BEVERAGES, APPETIZERS AND SOUPS

WINE IN VIRGINIA

Virginia has the longest winemaking history of the original thirteen English colonies. The Virginia Company even sent eight French vignerons to Jamestown in 1619 to get local viticulture off to a profitable start. The Jamestown Assembly passed "Acte 12" (commemorated in a Chardonnay by Williamsburg Winery), which compelled settlers to plant twelve wine grapevines yearly or suffer severe punishment. But the imported vines died, and native grapes produced "rath wine," so colonists focused on making a more profitable crop, tobacco.

The first English settlers found a profusion of native grape varieties and made wine; however, the earliest efforts did not produce satisfactory results. After Thomas Jefferson returned from his duties in France, he was convinced that wine would be a sound crop for Virginia farmers. Winemaking was often a common household activity, with scuppernong and other grape wines, blackberry, and cherry the most popular wines.

In the 1970s, a return to Virginia's colonial winemaking roots was undertaken; Virginia has fifty-three farm wineries scattered throughout the state. Today the Virginia wine industry combines the tradition of Europe, the technological expertise of California, and the zeal of its wine-growing pioneers to realize Jefferson's dream of a successful Virginia wine industry.

A History of Virginia Wine: A Summary
Richard Leahy

OPEN HOUSE PUNCH

2 cups water
2 cups sugar
1 (46-ounce) can apricot nectar, chilled
1 (46-ounce) can pineapple juice, chilled
1½ cups lemon juice, chilled
1 (6-ounce) can frozen orange juice concentrate, prepared, chilled
2 quarts ginger ale, chilled

Combine the water and sugar in a saucepan and mix well. Heat until the sugar dissolves, stirring occasionally. Let stand until cool. Chill in the refrigerator.

Pour the sugar mixture into a punch bowl. Stir in the apricot nectar, pineapple juice, lemon juice and orange juice. Add the ginger ale and mix well. Ladle into punch cups. *Yield: 50 servings.*

Approx Per Serving: Cal 81; Prot <1 g; Carbo 21 g; T Fat <1 g; 1% Calories from Fat; Chol 0 mg; Fiber <1 g; Sod 4 mg; Vit A 36 RE; Vit C 11 mg; Ca 9 mg; Iron <1 mg

PARTY PUNCH

2 quarts cranberry juice, chilled
2 quarts ginger ale, chilled
½ gallon orange sherbet

Combine the cranberry juice and ginger ale in a punch bowl and mix well. Fold in the orange sherbet. Ladle into punch cups. *Yield: 30 servings.*

Approx Per Serving: Cal 133; Prot 1 g; Carbo 31 g; T Fat 1 g; 7% Calories from Fat; Chol 3 mg; Fiber <1 g; Sod 30 mg; Vit A 8 RE; Vit C 26 mg; Ca 32 mg; Iron <1 mg

Fruited Ice Mold

Arrange sliced peaches and strawberry halves over the bottom of a 1-quart mold. Add just enough fruit juice to cover the fruit. Freeze until set. Add enough juice to fill the mold half full and freeze until set. Repeat the process. Add to your favorite punch.

SPECIAL PARTY PUNCH

2	(25-ounce) bottles sauterne, chilled	¾	cup superfine sugar
6	cups pineapple juice, chilled	½	cup lemon juice, chilled
		1	(1-liter) bottle club soda, chilled

Combine the wine, pineapple juice, sugar and lemon juice in a punch bowl and mix until the sugar dissolves. Stir in the club soda. Ladle into punch cups. *Yield: 16 servings.*

Approx Per Serving: Cal 151; Prot <1 g; Carbo 24 g; T Fat <1 g; 0% Calories from Fat; Chol 0 mg; Fiber <1 g; Sod 19 mg; Vit A 1 RE; Vit C 14 mg; Ca 28 mg; Iron 1 mg

PINEAPPLE PUNCH

2	quarts ginger ale, chilled	1	quart apple juice, chilled
1	quart pineapple juice, chilled	1	quart orange juice, chilled
		1	quart pineapple sherbet

Combine the ginger ale, pineapple juice, apple juice and orange juice in a punch bowl and mix well. Add the sherbet and mix gently. Ladle into punch cups. *Yield: 50 servings.*

Approx Per Serving: Cal 65; Prot <1 g; Carbo 15 g; T Fat <1 g; 5% Calories from Fat; Chol 1 mg; Fiber <1 g; Sod 11 mg; Vit A 6 RE; Vit C 13 mg; Ca 17 mg; Iron <1 mg

Pineapple Orange Cooler

1½ cups unsweetened
    pineapple juice
1½ cups orange juice
2 tablespoons lemon juice

1¼ cups seltzer water
4 thin orange slices
    (optional)

Combine the pineapple juice, orange juice and lemon juice in a 2-quart pitcher and mix well. Pour equal amounts of the juice mixture into four 12-ounce ice-filled glasses. Add the seltzer water and stir. Garnish each glass with an orange slice. *Yield: 4 servings.*

Approx Per Serving: Cal 96; Prot 1 g; Carbo 23 g; T Fat <1 g; 2% Calories from Fat; Chol 0 mg; Fiber <1 g; Sod 2 mg; Vit A 19 RE; Vit C 60 mg; Ca 27 mg; Iron <1 mg

Sangria

1 quart dry red wine
2 cups orange juice
½ cup sugar

½ cup orange liqueur
2 tablespoons lemon juice
1 orange, cut into 6 slices

Combine the red wine, orange juice, sugar, liqueur and lemon juice in a pitcher, stirring until the sugar dissolves. Pour over crushed ice in glasses. Top each with an orange slice. You may substitute any fresh fruit for the orange. *Yield: 6 servings.*

Approx Per Serving: Cal 304; Prot 1 g; Carbo 42 g; T Fat <1 g; 1% Calories from Fat; Chol 0 mg; Fiber 1 g; Sod 11 mg; Vit A 21 RE; Vit C 55 mg; Ca 31 mg; Iron 1 mg

Wine and beer, and—later—cider were popular drinks during the early colonial days. It was recommended by the colony assembly that all newcomers bring in a supply of malt to be used for these beverages until their bodies had become "hardened" to the land.

Homemade Lemonade

Combine the juice of 12 lemons with ½ cup sugar in a pitcher, stirring until the sugar dissolves. Cut the lemon peel into strips and add to the lemon mixture. Fill the pitcher with ice. Let stand at room temperature for 30 minutes to allow the ice to melt. Pour the lemonade over crushed ice in glasses. Garnish with lemon slices and sprigs of fresh mint.

HOT SPICED TEA

1½ cups sugar	6 tablespoons sweetened lemonade mix
¾ cup instant tea granules	1 teaspoon cinnamon
⅔ cup orange instant breakfast drink mix	½ teaspoon ground cloves

Combine the sugar, tea granules, breakfast drink mix, lemonade mix, cinnamon and cloves in a bowl and mix well. Store in an airtight container. Mix 1 level tablespoon of the tea mixture with 1 cup boiling water in a mug for each serving. *Yield: 54 servings.*

Approx Per Serving: Cal 45; Prot <1 g; Carbo 12 g; T Fat 0 g; 0% Calories from Fat; Chol 0 mg; Fiber <1 g; Sod 1 mg; Vit A 28 RE; Vit C 12 mg; Ca 18 mg; Iron <1 mg

WASSAIL

6 cinnamon sticks	2 cups cranberry juice
16 whole cloves	¼ cup sugar
1 teaspoon ground allspice	1 teaspoon bitters
6 cups water	¼ cup rum (optional)
1 (12-ounce) can frozen apple juice concentrate	

Tie the cinnamon sticks, cloves and allspice in a cheesecloth bag. Mix the water and apple juice concentrate in a saucepan. Stir in the cranberry juice, sugar and bitters. Add the spice bag. Bring to a simmer.

Simmer for 10 minutes, stirring occasionally. Discard the spice bag. Stir in the rum. Ladle into mugs. *Yield: 8 servings.*

Approx Per Serving: Cal 132; Prot <1 g; Carbo 33 g; T Fat <1 g; 1% Calories from Fat; Chol 0 mg; Fiber <1 g; Sod 12 mg; Vit A <1 RE; Vit C 23 mg; Ca 10 mg; Iron <1 mg

Nacho Dip

8 ounces nonfat cream cheese, softened	1 (4-ounce) can chopped green chiles, drained
1 (15-ounce) can turkey chili without beans	8 ounces taco cheese, shredded
4 green onions, minced	

Layer the cream cheese, chili, green onions, chiles and cheese in the order listed in an 8x8-inch or 9x9-inch baking pan. Bake at 350 degrees for 20 to 30 minutes or until bubbly. Serve with tortilla chips.

You may substitute your favorite reduced-fat cheese or a mixture of Monterey Jack cheese and Cheddar cheese for the taco cheese. If you use reduced-fat cheese, cover the baking pan with foil during the baking process. *Yield: 16 servings.*

Approx Per Serving: Cal 87; Prot 7 g; Carbo 3 g; T Fat 4 g; 50% Calories from Fat; Chol 20 mg; Fiber 1 g; Sod 415 mg; Vit A 95 RE; Vit C 5 mg; Ca 138 mg; Iron <1 mg

Tangy Cheese Balls

12 ounces cream cheese, softened	8 ounces extra-sharp Cheddar cheese, shredded
6 ounces bleu cheese or Roquefort cheese, crumbled	3/4 cup chopped pecans
	3/4 cup chopped fresh parsley
	1 garlic clove, minced

Beat the cream cheese in a mixing bowl at medium speed until creamy, scraping the bowl occasionally. Add the bleu cheese and Cheddar cheese. Beat until blended. Fold in 1/2 cup of the pecans, 1/2 cup of the parsley and garlic. Shape the mixture into 2 balls. Chill, wrapped in plastic wrap, for 8 to 10 hours. Roll the cheese balls in the remaining 1/4 cup pecans and 1/4 cup parsley. Serve with assorted party crackers. *Yield: 50 servings.*

Approx Per Serving: Cal 66; Prot 3 g; Carbo 1 g; T Fat 6 g; 81% Calories from Fat; Chol 15 mg; Fiber <1 g; Sod 97 mg; Vit A 57 RE; Vit C 1 mg; Ca 58 mg; Iron <1 mg

During the Civil War, or the War Between the States, soldiers would grind dried beans to brew as coffee. Potatoes were dried and ground to be used in place of wheat flour, and peach leaves were brewed into an infusion that was substituted for almond flavoring. Recipes from this era are almost unknown due to the scarcity of food and the temporary receipts improvised to prepare the available foods.

Swedish Nuts

Beat 2 egg whites in a mixing bowl until frothy. Add 1 cup sugar gradually and beat constantly until stiff peaks form. Fold in 1 pound salted mixed nuts. Heat 1/2 cup butter or margarine in a baking pan until melted. Spread the nut mixture in the prepared pan. Bake at 300 degrees for 30 minutes, stirring every 10 minutes. Spread on waxed paper. Let stand until cool. Separate into bite-size pieces. Store in an airtight container. Do not refrigerate. Yield: 3 cups.

HOT CRAB AND SHRIMP SPREAD

1   **(6-ounce) can crab meat, drained, flaked**
6   **to 8 ounces frozen popcorn shrimp, thawed, drained, chopped**
•   **Juice of 1 lemon**
1   **cup reduced-fat mayonnaise**

1   **teaspoon Worcestershire sauce**
1/2   **teaspoon Tabasco sauce**
1/8   **teaspoon salt**
1/8   **teaspoon pepper**
12   **butter crackers, crushed**

Combine the crab meat, shrimp and lemon juice in a bowl and mix well. Let stand at room temperature for 20 minutes, stirring occasionally.

Combine the mayonnaise, Worcestershire sauce and Tabasco sauce in a bowl and mix well. Stir in the salt and pepper. Add the crab meat mixture and mix well. Spoon into a 9-inch round baking pan. Sprinkle with the cracker crumbs.

Bake at 325 degrees for 20 to 25 minutes or until bubbly. Serve hot or cold with assorted party crackers, melba toast and/or toast points. *Yield: 20 servings.*

Approx Per Serving: Cal 50; Prot 3 g; Carbo 3 g; T Fat 3 g; 51% Calories from Fat; Chol 25 mg; Fiber <1 g; Sod 150 mg; Vit A <1 RE; Vit C 1 mg; Ca 9 mg; Iron <1 mg

Star City Ham Spread

8	ounces cream cheese, softened	1	tablespoon Worcestershire sauce
1	(3-ounce) jar minced ham	1	teaspoon prepared mustard
¼	cup chili sauce	1	teaspoon minced onion
2	tablespoons pickle relish	2	drops of Tabasco sauce
2	tablespoons minced fresh parsley		

Beat the cream cheese in a mixing bowl at medium speed until creamy, scraping the bowl occasionally. Stir in the ham, chili sauce, pickle relish, parsley, Worcestershire sauce, prepared mustard, onion and Tabasco sauce. Spoon into a crock. Serve with assorted party crackers. *Yield: 12 servings.*

Approx Per Serving: Cal 96; Prot 3 g; Carbo 3 g; T Fat 8 g; 75% Calories from Fat; Chol 26 mg; Fiber <1 g; Sod 261 mg; Vit A 84 RE; Vit C 2 mg; Ca 20 mg; Iron <1 mg

How much sodium is too much? Over 4000 milligrams. This amount is very easy to attain, considering the following:
* *One teaspoon of salt has 2000 milligrams of sodium*
* *One pickle has almost 1000 milligrams of sodium*
* *One-half can of most canned soups has 800 milligrams of sodium*

Look at the "Nutrition Facts" on food labels for the amount of sodium the product contains. Check the ingredients list for "hidden" sodium: MSG, sodium alginate, sodium benzoate, sodium propionate, sodium caseinate, sodium chloride, sodium nitrate, sodium bisulfite, disodium inosinate, baking soda, baking powder, onion salt, garlic salt, salt brine, and soy sauce.

HUMMUS

An adaptation of the traditional Middle Eastern purée of chick-peas.

1	(15-ounce) can chick-peas	2	garlic cloves
2	tablespoons lemon juice	1/4	teaspoon cumin
1	tablespoon minced onion	1/8	teaspoon cayenne pepper
1	teaspoon tahini		

Drain the chick-peas, reserving the liquid. Combine the chick-peas, lemon juice, onion, tahini, garlic, cumin and cayenne pepper in a blender container. Process until smooth. Add just enough of the reserved liquid to make to your desired consistency and mix well.

Use as a sandwich spread with lettuce, tomato, cucumber, green bell peppers and sprouts on whole wheat pita bread or serve as a dip with fresh vegetables or chips. *Yield: 4 (1/3-cup) servings.*

Approx Per Serving: Cal 141; Prot 6 g; Carbo 26 g; T Fat 2 g; 13% Calories from Fat; Chol 0 mg; Fiber 5 g; Sod 319 mg; Vit A 2 RE; Vit C 9 mg; Ca 41 mg; Iron 2 mg

Salmon Ball

1	(15-ounce) can red Alaskan salmon	2	teaspoons grated onion
8	ounces cream cheese, softened	1	teaspoon prepared horseradish
1	tablespoon lemon juice	¼	teaspoon liquid smoke
		⅓	cup chopped fresh parsley

Drain the salmon and discard the skin and bones. Combine the salmon, cream cheese, lemon juice, onion, horseradish and liquid smoke in a bowl and mix well. Shape the salmon mixture into a ball. Chill, wrapped in plastic wrap, for 8 to 10 hours.

Coat the ball with the parsley. Garnish with lemon wedges and/or black olives. Serve with assorted party crackers. You may pack the salmon mixture into a mold lined with plastic wrap. Substitute chopped nuts for the parsley if desired. *Yield: 24 servings.*

Approx Per Serving: Cal 65; Prot 4 g; Carbo <1 g; T Fat 5 g; 71% Calories from Fat; Chol 22 mg; Fiber <1 g; Sod 105 mg; Vit A 49 RE; Vit C 2 mg; Ca 37 mg; Iron <1 mg

Canned fish such as salmon and sardines are good sources of calcium because the bones are never removed before the canning process.

Spinach Soy Slices

1	(10-ounce) package frozen chopped spinach, thawed, drained	¼	teaspoon garlic powder
1	(10-ounce) package silken tofu, drained, chopped	¼	teaspoon salt
		1	cup coarsely shredded carrots
1	tablespoon lemon juice	¼	cup chopped green onions (optional)
¾	teaspoon onion powder	1	baguette, sliced
½	teaspoon tarragon	¼	cup grated soy Parmesan cheese

Press the spinach to remove the excess moisture. Combine the tofu and lemon juice in a blender container. Process until smooth. Add the onion powder, tarragon, garlic powder and salt. Process just until blended.

Spoon the tofu mixture into a bowl. Add the spinach, carrots and green onions and mix well. Spread on the bread slices. Arrange on a baking sheet. Sprinkle with the soy cheese. Broil just until the slices start to brown. *Yield: 20 servings.*

Approx Per Serving: Cal 25; Prot 2 g; Carbo 3 g; T Fat 1 g; 28% Calories from Fat; Chol 0 mg; Fiber 1 g; Sod 73 mg; Vit A 265 RE; Vit C 4 mg; Ca 22 mg; Iron 1 mg

Stuffed French Bread

1	loaf French bread	½	cup sour cream
2	or 3 garlic cloves, minced	1	(15-ounce) can artichoke
1	tablespoon butter		hearts, drained, chopped
1	cup shredded Monterey		
	Jack cheese		

Cut the bread lengthwise into halves. Remove the centers carefully, leaving the shells intact. Crumble the bread.

Sauté the garlic in the butter in a skillet. Combine the garlic, crumbled bread, cheese, sour cream and artichokes in a bowl and mix well. Spoon into the bread shells. Fit the shells together to form a loaf and wrap in foil. Place on a baking sheet.

Bake at 350 degrees for 15 to 20 minutes or until heated through. Slice and serve immediately. May be frozen unbaked for future use. Thaw before baking. Reduce the fat content by using reduced-fat cheese and sour cream.
Yield: 12 servings.

Approx Per Serving: Cal 184; Prot 7 g; Carbo 23 g; T Fat 7 g; 34% Calories from Fat; Chol 15 mg; Fiber 2 g; Sod 399 mg; Vit A 51 RE; Vit C 2 mg; Ca 111 mg; Iron 2 mg

Caffeine content of 6- to 8-ounce servings of the following beverages is as follows: brewed coffee, 103 to 175 mg; instant coffee, 57 to 79 mg; decaffeinated coffee, 2 to 5 mg; tea (1- to 5-minute brew time), 36 to 59 mg; instant tea, 25 to 36 mg; colas, 40 to 65 mg; hot cocoa, 11 mg.

Try these healthy
quick and easy snacks.
Make your own gorp
by combining your
favorite cereals, dried
fruit, pretzels, dried
seeds, and nut mixes.
Eliminate or reduce the
amount of nuts added
to the mix to reduce
fat grams and calories.
Serve air-popped
popcorn sprinkled with
grated Parmesan cheese
for a healthy quick and
easy snack.

GRAB-N-GO GORP

Great snack for children and adults. High in fiber, vitamins, minerals and protein.

2	cups wheat Chex	1	cup dried blueberries
2	cups mixed nuts	1	cup semisweet chocolate
1	cup dried cherries		chips
1	cup dried cranberries		

Combine the cereal, mixed nuts, cherries, cranberries, blueberries and chocolate chips in a bowl and mix well. Store in an airtight container. *Yield: 16 (¹/₂-cup) servings.*

Approx Per Serving: Cal 277; Prot 5 g; Carbo 41 g; T Fat 14 g; 40% Calories from Fat; Chol <1 mg; Fiber 5 g; Sod 157 mg; Vit A 51 RE; Vit C 15 mg; Ca 38 mg; Iron 4 mg

SOYBEAN GRANOLA

This is a great snack for individuals requiring gluten-free diets.

4	cups puffed rice cereal	1	cup roasted soybeans
1	cup textured vegetable protein	1	cup raisins (optional)
		¹/₂	cup rice flour
1	cup sliced almonds or other nuts	¹/₂	cup honey
		¹/₄	cup vegetable oil
1	cup sunflower seed kernels	1	teaspoon vanilla extract

Mix the first seven ingredients in a bowl. Combine the honey, oil and vanilla in a saucepan and mix well. Bring to a boil, stirring frequently.

Pour the honey mixture over the cereal mixture and toss to coat. Spread the cereal mixture in a single layer on 2 greased baking sheets. Toast at 325 degrees for 15 minutes or until golden brown, stirring occasionally. *Yield: 16 (¹/₂-cup) servings.*

Approx Per Serving: Cal 269; Prot 14 g; Carbo 26 g; T Fat 15 g; 45% Calories from Fat; Chol 0 mg; Fiber 6 g; Sod 3 mg; Vit A 3 RE; Vit C 1 mg; Ca 77 mg; Iron 4 mg

BLT Soup

8	slices lean bacon, cut into 1-inch pieces	1/2	teaspoon garlic salt
1/3	cup chopped onion	1/2	teaspoon parsley flakes
1/3	cup chopped celery	1/4	teaspoon whole thyme
5	or 6 tomatoes, peeled, coarsely chopped	1/4	teaspoon pepper
4	cups beef broth	1/8	teaspoon hot sauce
1	tablespoon Worcestershire sauce	2 1/2	to 3 cups shredded leaf lettuce
		1/3	cup seasoned croutons

Fry the bacon in a large saucepan until crisp. Drain the bacon, reserving 2 tablespoons of the drippings. Pat the bacon with paper towels to remove excess drippings.

Sauté the onion and celery in the reserved drippings in the saucepan until tender. Add half the bacon, tomatoes, broth, Worcestershire sauce, garlic salt, parsley flakes, thyme, pepper and hot sauce to the onion mixture and mix well. Bring to a boil; reduce heat.

Simmer for 20 to 25 minutes, stirring occasionally. Stir in the lettuce. Cook for 2 minutes or until the lettuce wilts, stirring occasionally. Ladle into soup bowls. Top with the remaining bacon and croutons. Serve immediately. Do not substitute iceberg lettuce for the leaf lettuce.
Yield: 5 (1-cup) servings.

Approx Per Serving: Cal 129; Prot 7 g; Carbo 12 g; T Fat 7 g; 43% Calories from Fat; Chol 9 mg; Fiber 3 g; Sod 1059 mg; Vit A 158 RE; Vit C 36 mg; Ca 55 mg; Iron 2 mg

Most people require at least eight glasses of water daily. Water sources include tap water, bottled water, beverages, soups, gelatin, and ice cubes. Many water-based drinks like coffee and carbonated beverages that contain caffeine and sugar can cause water loss. They can slow absorption and delay rehydration.

Hearty Bean and Tomato Soup

Warm up this fall with a hearty bean soup that is easy to prepare. This soup is loaded with flavor and fiber and very little fat. Serve with a green salad and whole grain rolls.

To make savory broths for seafood-based soups or pasta sauces, simmer equal amounts of clam juice and water with dry white wine (not cooking wine), chopped green onions, dillweed, parsley, and thyme for thirty minutes and strain. To enhance the flavor of canned reduced-sodium chicken broth, add a splash of vinegar or lemon juice and the desired amount of chopped fresh parsley.

³/₄ cup chopped onion	2 cups coarsely chopped
2 garlic cloves, minced	fresh spinach, kale, Swiss
1 teaspoon vegetable oil	chard or bok choy
3 cups water	1 cup quick-cooking
1 (15-ounce) can kidney	brown rice
beans, drained, rinsed	2 teaspoons basil
1 (15-ounce) can garbanzos,	1 teaspoon oregano
Great Northern beans or	¹/₄ teaspoon pepper
cannellini, drained, rinsed	3 tablespoons grated
2 cups tomato purée	Parmesan cheese
1 teaspoon reduced-sodium	(optional)
instant chicken bouillon	
granules	

Sauté the onion and garlic in the oil in a large saucepan for 2 minutes or until the onion is tender. Stir in the water, kidney beans, garbanzos, tomato purée, bouillon granules, spinach, brown rice, basil, oregano and pepper. Bring to a boil; reduce heat.

Simmer for 15 minutes or until the rice is tender, stirring occasionally. Ladle into soup bowls. Sprinkle with the cheese. Serve immediately.
Yield: 8 (1-cup) servings.

Approx Per Serving: Cal 208; Prot 9 g; Carbo 40 g; T Fat 2 g; 8% Calories from Fat; Chol 0 mg; Fiber 9 g; Sod 418 mg; Vit A 132 RE; Vit C 12 mg; Ca 39 mg; Iron 2 mg

BEVERAGES, APPETIZERS AND SOUPS

Black Bean and Corn Soup

12	ounces lean ground round	1	(14-ounce) can diced tomatoes
2	(15-ounce) cans black beans, drained, rinsed	1	(14-ounce) can beef broth
2	cups frozen whole kernel corn	1	tablespoon chili powder
		1	teaspoon cumin

Brown the ground round in a saucepan, stirring until crumbly; drain. Stir in the beans, corn, undrained tomatoes, broth, chili powder and cumin. Bring to a boil; reduce heat.

Simmer, covered, for 15 minutes, stirring occasionally. Ladle into soup bowls. *Yield: 6 (1-cup) servings.*

Approx Per Serving: Cal 310; Prot 24 g; Carbo 33 g; T Fat 10 g; 29% Calories from Fat; Chol 41 mg; Fiber 10 g; Sod 1106 mg; Vit A 77 RE; Vit C 13 mg; Ca 63 mg; Iron 5 mg

Black beans are a good source of soluble fiber and protein. Soluble fiber decreases cholesterol and triglycerides, protects against colon cancer, helps to control blood pressure, and reduces constipation. One-half cup of cooked black beans contains nine and one-half grams of fiber and seven grams of protein.

BEEF VEGETABLE SOUP

Reduce the fat content of browned ground beef by following these simple steps. Remove the browned ground beef to a platter lined with white paper towels. Let stand for 1 minute, blotting the top of the ground beef with additional paper towels. Transfer the ground beef to a fine mesh strainer or colander. Pour 4 cups hot (not boiling) water over the ground beef. Drain for 5 minutes. Wipe the skillet clean with a paper towel. Return the drained ground beef to the skillet. Proceed as the recipe directs.

1	pound lean ground beef	2	beef bouillon cubes
2	onions, finely chopped	1	tablespoon sugar
4	ribs celery with leaves, chopped	½	teaspoon parsley flakes
4	cups water	½	teaspoon thyme
1	(16-ounce) package frozen mixed vegetables	½	teaspoon marjoram
¼	head cabbage, chopped	¼	teaspoon oregano
6	unpeeled potatoes, coarsely chopped	2	(28-ounce) cans diced tomatoes

Brown the ground beef in a large saucepan, stirring until crumbly; drain. Add the onions and celery and cook until tender-crisp, stirring frequently. Stir in the water, mixed vegetables, cabbage, potatoes, bouillon cubes, sugar, parsley flakes, thyme, marjoram and oregano.

Cook until the vegetables are tender, stirring occasionally. Add the undrained tomatoes and mix well. Bring to a boil; reduce heat to low. Simmer, covered, for 45 minutes, stirring occasionally. Ladle into soup bowls. *Yield: 15 (1-cup) servings.*

Approx Per Serving: Cal 162; Prot 11 g; Carbo 22 g; T Fat 5 g; 23% Calories from Fat; Chol 21 mg; Fiber 4 g; Sod 341 mg; Vit A 200 RE; Vit C 33 mg; Ca 49 mg; Iron 3 mg

CARROT SOUP

Great recipe for using leftover cooked carrots or boiled potatoes.

2	slices bacon	2	cups sliced carrots
¼	cup chopped onion	1	medium potato, peeled,
1	(28-ounce) can		chopped
	chicken broth	1	medium tomato, chopped

Fry the bacon in a saucepan until almost cooked through; drain. Chop the bacon. Return the bacon to the saucepan. Add the onion and sauté until the onion is tender. Stir in the broth, carrots, potato and tomato. Bring to a boil; reduce heat.

Simmer for 20 minutes or until the vegetables are tender, stirring occasionally. May process the soup in small amounts in a blender or food processor for a smooth consistency if desired. Cook just until heated through, stirring frequently. Ladle into soup bowls. *Yield: 4 (1-cup) servings.*

Approx Per Serving: Cal 141; Prot 12 g; Carbo 16 g; T Fat 4 g; 24% Calories from Fat; Chol 5 mg; Fiber 3 g; Sod 1317 mg; Vit A 1735 RE; Vit C 19 mg; Ca 37 mg; Iron 2 mg

Phytochemicals are substances found in foods that are important for the prevention of disease. Like antioxidants, they are not an energy substance but are important for reactions in the body. Foods rich in phytochemicals are brown rice, oats, whole wheat, dry beans, tofu products, apples, berries, melons, citrus, grapes, broccoli, cabbage, carrots, cauliflower, celery, cucumbers, potatoes, eggplant, onions, peppers, tomatoes, and turnips, spices and herbs like garlic, ginger, turmeric, oregano, basil, mint, chives, thyme, rosemary, tarragon, and sage.

GAZPACHO

Recipe furnished by Belle Kuisine of Richmond, Virginia.

½ cup small bread cubes	1 tablespoon extra-virgin olive oil
1 tablespoon extra-virgin olive oil	4 tomatoes, chopped
2 cups chopped, seeded peeled cucumbers	3 cups tomato juice
3 scallion bulbs, chopped	1 tablespoon extra-virgin olive oil
1 small green bell pepper, chopped	½ teaspoon salt (optional)
1 small red bell pepper, chopped	¼ teaspoon freshly ground pepper, or to taste
2 tablespoons chopped fresh basil	1 tablespoon balsamic vinegar, or to taste
1 tablespoon fresh lime juice	

Toss the bread cubes with 1 tablespoon olive oil in a bowl. Spread in a single layer on an ungreased baking sheet. Toast at 400 degrees for 5 minutes or until crisp.

Combine the bread cubes, ½ of the cucumbers, ½ of the scallions, ½ of the bell peppers, basil, ½ of the lime juice and 1 tablespoon olive oil in a bowl and mix well. Set aside.

Combine the remaining cucumbers, remaining scallions, remaining bell peppers, remaining lime juice, tomatoes and tomato juice in a food processor container. Process for 1 minute or until smooth.

Pour the soup into a bowl. Stir in 1 tablespoon olive oil, salt and pepper. Ladle into chilled soup bowls. Top each serving with ¼ of the vegetable mixture and drizzle with the balsamic vinegar just before serving. *Yield: 4 servings.*

Approx Per Serving: Cal 185; Prot 4 g; Carbo 22 g; T Fat 11 g; 49% Calories from Fat; Chol <1 mg; Fiber 4 g; Sod 691 mg; Vit A 329 RE; Vit C 124 mg; Ca 44 mg; Iron 2 mg

Clam Chowder

Clam Chowder is a hearty thick soup that is usually made with a milk or cream base. New England clam chowder is prepared with clams, salt pork or bacon, milk, and seasonings, while Virginia clam chowder incorporates water, clam or crab broth, potatoes, onion and a variety of herbs and spices. Milk may or may not be added to the chowder. Evaporated skim milk was used instead of cream in this recipe to reduce fat grams and make for a healthier soup.

¼ cup (½ stick) butter	• Salt and white pepper to taste
2 (8-ounce) cans minced clams	2 tablespoons cornmeal or flour
2 (8-ounce) bottles clam juice	1 cup evaporated skim milk
3 medium potatoes, peeled, coarsely chopped	¼ cup sherry (optional)
1 onion, finely chopped	½ teaspoon chopped fresh parsley

Heat the butter in a saucepan until melted. Add the undrained clams, clam juice, potatoes and onion and mix well. Simmer until the potatoes are tender, stirring occasionally. Season with salt and white pepper.

Combine the cornmeal with enough water in a bowl to make a paste. Stir into the clam mixture. Add the evaporated skim milk and sherry and mix well. Cook just until heated through, stirring frequently; do not boil.

Ladle into soup bowls. Sprinkle with the parsley. May substitute 12 cooked fresh shucked clams for the canned clams. Strain the cooking liquid and add enough water to measure 4 cups. *Yield: 4 servings.*

Approx Per Serving: Cal 344; Prot 25 g; Carbo 35 g; T Fat 13 g; 33% Calories from Fat; Chol 74 mg; Fiber 3 g; Sod 619 mg; Vit A 287 RE; Vit C 25 mg; Ca 273 mg; Iron 18 mg

Food sources rich in calcium include the following: 1 cup skim milk contains 300 mg calcium; 1 cup buttermilk contains 285 mg calcium; 1 cup 2% cottage cheese contains 205 mg calcium; 1 cup plain low-fat yogurt contains 415 mg calcium; 1 cup plain nonfat yogurt contains 452 mg calcium; 1 cup low-fat fruit yogurt contains 345 mg calcium; 1 cup ice cream contains 190 mg calcium; 6 ounces hard cheese contains 130 mg calcium; and 6 ounces soft cheese contains 160 mg calcium.

RED LENTIL AND RICE SOUP

1	cup dried red lentils	2	teaspoons vegetable oil
2	carrots, finely chopped	2	teaspoons cumin
1	onion, finely chopped	7	cups vegetable broth
2	garlic cloves, finely chopped	¼	cup white rice
		•	Pepper to taste

Sort and rinse the lentils. Sauté the carrots, onion and garlic in the oil in a large saucepan for 2 to 3 minutes. Stir in the cumin. Sauté for 1 minute longer.

Add the lentils, broth and rice to the carrot mixture and mix well. Simmer for 20 minutes or until the rice is tender, stirring occasionally. Season with pepper. Ladle into soup bowls. *Yield: 8 (1-cup) servings.*

Approx Per Serving: Cal 135; Prot 8 g; Carbo 23 g; T Fat 2 g; 14% Calories from Fat; Chol 0 mg; Fiber 6 g; Sod 883 mg; Vit A 524 RE; Vit C 4 mg; Ca 22 mg; Iron 2 mg

Hearty Lentil and Barley Soup

³⁄₄	cup dried lentils	¹⁄₂	cup pearl barley
1	cup chopped onion	¹⁄₂	cup chopped frozen green
1	cup chopped celery		beans, thawed
¹⁄₂	cup chopped carrot	1	cup chopped zucchini
1	teaspoon vegetable oil	1	cup elbow macaroni
8	to 9 cups chicken or	2	tablespoons chopped fresh
	vegetable broth		dillweed or thyme
1	cup chopped potato	•	Salt and pepper to taste
1	cup fresh or canned		
	chopped tomato		

Sort and rinse the lentils. Sauté the onion, celery and carrot in the oil in a stockpot until the vegetables are tender-crisp. Add the broth and mix well. Stir in the lentils, potato, tomato and barley. Bring to a simmer over medium heat; reduce heat.

Simmer, covered, over low heat for 30 minutes, stirring occasionally. Add the green beans, zucchini and macaroni and mix well. Cook for 15 minutes or until the macaroni is tender, stirring occasionally. Stir in the dillweed, salt and pepper. Ladle into soup bowls. *Yield: 12 (1-cup) servings.*

Approx Per Serving: Cal 156; Prot 9 g; Carbo 26 g; T Fat 2 g; 11% Calories from Fat; Chol 0 mg; Fiber 5 g; Sod 598 mg; Vit A 171 RE; Vit C 10 mg; Ca 32 mg; Iron 3 mg

Folate is considered one of the gene nutrients. It is important for genetic material in our cells and is needed as well to prevent certain types of anemia and neurological disorders. Folate is especially important for all women of child-bearing age. Over-supplementation of folate can hide B^{12} deficiencies, so always check with a dietitian or physician before taking single-nutrient supplements. The best sources of folate are as follows: barley, dried beans, fortified cereals and breads, fruits and fruit juices (orange juice), garbanzo beans, leafy green vegetables (spinach, kale, collard greens, turnip greens), lentils, liver, peas, soybeans, split peas and whole wheat.

Oyster Stew

1	pint oysters	•	**Pepper to taste**
2	tablespoons margarine	4	**cups milk**
³/₄	teaspoon salt	•	**Paprika to taste**
¹/₈	teaspoon Tabasco sauce		

Drain the oysters, reserving the liquor. Heat the margarine in a saucepan over medium heat until melted. Stir in the salt, Tabasco sauce and pepper. Add the reserved oyster liquor and mix well.

Stir in the oysters. Cook for 5 minutes or until the edges curl. Add the milk and mix well. Cook just until heated through, stirring occasionally; do not boil. Ladle into heated soup bowls. Sprinkle with paprika. You may substitute evaporated skim milk for the whole milk.

Yield: 6 (1-cup) servings.

Approx Per Serving: Cal 216; Prot 15 g; Carbo 13 g; T Fat 12 g; 49% Calories from Fat; Chol 72 mg; Fiber 0 g; Sod 522 mg; Vit A 162 RE; Vit C 8 mg; Ca 203 mg; Iron 5 mg

Split Pea Soup

2	cups dried green split peas	½	teaspoon thyme
1	cup chopped celery	½	teaspoon dry mustard
1	large carrot, sliced	1	bay leaf
⅔	cup chopped onion	•	Freshly ground pepper
1	large garlic clove, minced		to taste
3	tablespoons vegetable oil	1	cup chopped canned or
6	cups water		fresh tomato
1	large potato, cut into	3	tablespoons dry
	½-inch cubes		cooking wine
1	teaspoon basil	1	tablespoon vinegar
1	teaspoon oregano	1	tablespoon soy sauce

Sort and rinse the split peas. Sauté the celery, carrot, onion and garlic in the oil in a stockpot until the vegetables are tender. Stir in the split peas, water, potato, basil, oregano, thyme, dry mustard, bay leaf and pepper.

Cook for 45 to 60 minutes or until the split peas are tender, stirring occasionally. Stir in the tomato, wine, vinegar and soy sauce. Simmer for 15 minutes, stirring occasionally. Discard the bay leaf.

Process all or half of the soup depending on the consistency desired in a blender or food processor until puréed. Return to the stockpot. Cook just until heated through, stirring frequently. Ladle into soup bowls. May freeze for future use. *Yield: 9 (1-cup) servings.*

Approx Per Serving: Cal 204; Prot 10 g; Carbo 31 g; T Fat 5 g; 22% Calories from Fat; Chol <1 mg; Fiber 10 g; Sod 242 mg; Vit A 295 RE; Vit C 10 mg; Ca 34 mg; Iron 2 mg

Beef Tea

Old Receipt for the Invalid Soldier

Cut 3 pounds of beef into small pieces and chop up the bones, if any; put it into a kettle, with ½ pound of mixed vegetables, such as onions, leeks, celery, turnips, carrots (or one or two of these), if all are not to be obtained; 1 ounce of salt; a little pepper; 1 teaspoonful of sugar; 2 ounces of butter; ½ pint of water.

Set it on a sharp fire for ten minutes or a quarter of an hour, stirring now and then with a spoon till it forms a rather thick gravy at bottom, but not brown; then add 7 pints of hot or cold water, but hot is preferable; after boiling, let it simmer gently for an hour; skim off all the fat, strain it through a sieve, and serve.

Alexis Soyer (1861)

Peanut Soup

Peanuts came to America via Africa. Dr. George Washington Carver contributed much to southern agriculture through the discovery of the many uses of peanuts and soybeans. After boll weevils destroyed the cotton crop early in the twentieth century, southerners took Dr. Carver's advice and made peanuts their money crop.

Today the actual growing of peanuts is associated with Southside, Virginia, where the bushes thrive in the sandy soil, producing food for Virginia kitchens and fodder for feeding the hogs.

2	ribs celery, chopped		2	cups peanut butter
1	small onion, chopped		1	tablespoon lemon juice
½	cup (1 stick) butter		1	teaspoon salt
3	tablespoons flour		⅓	teaspoon celery salt
2	quarts chicken broth, heated		½	cup ground peanuts

Sauté the celery and onion in the butter in a saucepan for 5 minutes. Add the flour, stirring until mixed. Stir in the hot broth.

Cook for 30 minutes, stirring occasionally. Remove from heat. Strain, discarding the solids. Return the liquid to the saucepan. Stir in the peanut butter, lemon juice, salt and celery salt. Cook just until heated through, stirring frequently. Ladle into soup bowls. Sprinkle with the ground peanuts. *Yield: 10 (1-cup) servings.*

Approx Per Serving: Cal 507; Prot 21 g; Carbo 16 g; T Fat 43 g; 72% Calories from Fat; Chol 25 mg; Fiber 4 g; Sod 1244 mg; Vit A 87 RE; Vit C 2 mg; Ca 48 mg; Iron 2 mg

St. John's Church

© P. Buckley Moss, 1998

WILLIAMSBURG AND TIDEWATER HOSPITALITY

An Old Receipt for Virginia Ham

The following receipt for cooking Virginia ham, always on the table
as a "side dish," was written on the flyleaf of the Bible owned by the first
William Byrd of Westover, somewhere around the year 1674:

"To eat ye Ham in Perfection steep it in Half Milk and Half Water
for 36 hours, and then having brought the water to a boil put ye Ham
therein and let it simmer, not boil, for 4 to 5 hours according to Size of ye
Ham for simmering Brings ye salt out and boiling drives it in."

Hams from Virginia were always special. In the early colony, the hogs
were fed on a mixture of fruits and nuts from the oak, hickory, chestnut, beech, and
persimmon trees. The settlers learned how the Indians salt-cured and smoked
venison for preservation, and they adapted the process to pork.

Virginia ladies took great pride in the quality of their hams. Martha Washington
cured her own, and it was reported that one was boiled daily for guests at Mount Vernon.

ENTREES

Favorite Colonial Fish

Smithfield and Isle of Wight County were first occupied by the Warrasquoyackes, who were among the Indians friendly to the colonists; they gave Captain John Smith corn when his group was experiencing famine, and frequently traded with the colonists. The Indians taught the English to become fishermen for the colony and for export to Europe. John Egerton wrote that no meat, not even pork or game, goes back as far in the recorded history of America as fish. Favorites for the colonists were sturgeon, oysters, crabs, shrimp, catfish, flounder, and red snapper.

Shad
A favorite breakfast delicacy of the Tidewater area.

1 shad fillet
1 teaspoon lemon juice
Salt and pepper to taste
1 slice bacon

Place the shad on a piece of heavy-duty foil large enough to enclose. Drizzle with the lemon juice and sprinkle with salt and pepper. Arrange the bacon over the top and seal the foil to enclose the fish. Arrange the packet on a baking sheet. Bake at 375 degrees for 15 minutesor until the shad flakes easily, opening the foil during the end of the baking process to allow the fish to brown.

Yield: 1 serving

BEEF TENDERLOIN

¾	cup vegetable oil	1	teaspoon garlic powder
½	cup reduced-sodium soy sauce	1	teaspoon grated gingerroot
3	tablespoons honey	1	green onion, chopped
2	tablespoons vinegar	1	(5-pound) beef tenderloin, trimmed

Combine the oil, soy sauce, honey, vinegar, garlic powder, gingerroot and green onion in a bowl and mix well. Pour over the beef in a dish, turning to coat. Marinate, covered, in the refrigerator for 8 to 10 hours. Drain, reserving half the marinade.

Place the beef in a 9x13-inch baking pan. Pour the reserved marinade over the beef. Bake at 400 degrees for 40 minutes or until of the desired degree of doneness. *Yield: 20 servings.*

Approx Per Serving: Cal 265; Prot 24 g; Carbo 4 g; T Fat 17 g; 57% Calories from Fat; Chol 70 mg; Fiber <1 g; Sod 255 mg; Vit A <1 RE; Vit C <1 mg; Ca 8 mg; Iron 3 mg
Nutritional information includes the entire amount of marinade.

Trim away any visible fat on meat and poultry. Even on lean cuts of meat, you will find some fat. Trimming the fat removes some, but not all, the cholesterol because cholesterol is in both the lean tissue and fat in meat, poultry, and fish. On whole birds, be sure to remove the fat near the opening of the cavity.

GRILLED HERB MUSTARD STEAKS

Try the Herb Mustard Sauce on chicken, pork chops, or tuna.

Herb Mustard Sauce

2	large garlic cloves, crushed	1	teaspoon basil
2	teaspoons water	½	teaspoon pepper
2	tablespoons Dijon mustard	½	teaspoon thyme

Steaks

4	(6-ounce) boneless beef top loin steaks or rib-eye steaks, 1 inch thick	•	Salt to taste

For the sauce, combine the garlic and water in a 1-cup microwave-safe measuring cup. Microwave on High for 30 seconds. Stir in the Dijon mustard, basil, pepper and thyme.

For the steaks, spread the mustard sauce on both sides of the steaks. Place the steaks on a grill rack over medium-hot coals. Grill the top loin steaks for 15 to 18 minutes or the rib-eye steaks for 11 to 14 minutes for medium-rare to medium, turning occasionally. Season with salt. Cut each steak crosswise into thick slices. *Yield: 4 servings.*

Approx Per Serving: Cal 258; Prot 39 g; Carbo 1 g; T Fat 10 g; 35% Calories from Fat; Chol 112 mg; Fiber <1 g; Sod 273 mg; Vit A 0 RE; Vit C 1 mg; Ca 28 mg; Iron 4 mg

Thai Beef Grill

Peanut Sauce

2 tablespoons light teriyaki sauce

2 tablespoons creamy peanut butter

2 tablespoons water

1/4 teaspoon crushed red pepper

Steaks

2 (8-ounce) boneless beef top loin or top sirloin steaks, 1 inch thick

1 large Vidalia, Walla Walla or Texas Sweet onion, cut into 1/2-inch slices

3 tablespoons light teriyaki sauce

For the sauce, combine the teriyaki sauce, peanut butter and water in a bowl, stirring with a fork until smooth. Add the red pepper and mix well.

For the steaks, brush both sides of the steaks and onion slices with the teriyaki sauce. Arrange the steaks and onion slices on a grill rack over medium-hot coals. Grill the top loin steaks for 15 to 18 minutes or the sirloin steaks for 17 to 21 minutes or until medium-rare to medium and until the onion is tender, turning occasionally. You may broil the steaks for approximately half the grilling time if desired.

To serve, trim the fat from the steaks. Cut each steak diagonally into thick slices. Serve with the sauce and sliced onion. *Yield: 4 servings.*

Approx Per Serving: Cal 247; Prot 29 g; Carbo 9 g; T Fat 10 g; 38% Calories from Fat; Chol 75 mg; Fiber 1 g; Sod 642 mg; Vit A 0 RE; Vit C 2 mg; Ca 20 mg; Iron 4 mg

Iron, a required mineral for good health, transports oxygen to all the cells and tissues in the body. Iron deficiency can lead to anemia, weakness, reduced capacity to work, and lowered resistance to infection. Animal-type foods, such as lean and trimmed meats, egg yolks, liver, poultry, and seafood, are the best sources of easily absorbed iron. Foods of plant origin that are rich in iron include enriched breads and cereals, enriched pasta and rice, dried beans and peas, green leafy vegetables, and dried fruits.

Plum Good Tenderloin

1 (2½-pound) pork tenderloin	• Salt and pepper to taste
2 tablespoons butter, softened	1 (12-ounce) jar plum preserves
¼ cup flour	½ cup Dijon mustard

Rub the surface of the pork with the butter. Coat with a mixture of the flour, salt and pepper. Arrange the pork in a baking pan. Bake at 350 degrees for about 35 minutes per pound. Cut into 1-inch slices.

Arrange the slices in a 9x12-inch baking dish. Combine the preserves and Dijon mustard in a bowl and mix well. Spread over the pork. Bake, covered with foil, for 30 minutes longer or until heated through.
Yield: 12 servings.

Approx Per Serving: Cal 224; Prot 21 g; Carbo 21 g; T Fat 6 g; 25% Calories from Fat; Chol 61 mg; Fiber 1 g; Sod 323 mg; Vit A 20 RE; Vit C 3 mg; Ca 25 mg; Iron 2 mg

Marinated Roast Pork

1 tablespoon olive oil
1 tablespoon Dijon mustard
2 teaspoons chopped fresh rosemary
2 garlic cloves, crushed
• Salt and pepper to taste
1 (1½-pound) boneless pork loin roast

¼ cup Dijon mustard
3 tablespoons water
3 tablespoons olive oil
1 tablespoon lemon juice
1 tablespoon drained capers

Whisk 1 tablespoon olive oil, 1 tablespoon Dijon mustard, rosemary, garlic, salt and pepper in a bowl until mixed. Brush the surface of the pork with the olive oil mixture. Place in a roasting pan.

Roast at 350 degrees for 1½ hours or until a meat thermometer registers 160 degrees. Let stand until cool. Cut the pork into thin slices. Arrange in a dish.

Whisk ¼ cup Dijon mustard, water, 3 tablespoons olive oil and lemon juice in a bowl until smooth. Stir in the capers. Pour over the pork, turning to coat.

Marinate in the refrigerator for 1 hour, turning occasionally. Arrange the pork on a platter. Drizzle with any remaining marinade. May serve chilled or heat if desired. *Yield: 6 servings.*

Approx Per Serving: Cal 275; Prot 25 g; Carbo 2 g; T Fat 18 g; 60% Calories from Fat; Chol 69 mg; Fiber <1 g; Sod 365 mg; Vit A 2 RE; Vit C 2 mg; Ca 35 mg; Iron 1 mg
Nutritional information includes the entire amount of marinade.

Use a small spray bottle filled with vegetable oil for a light spritz when frying, baking, or tossing salads.

ORIENTAL PORK ROAST

Pork

1	**(4- to 5-pound) tied rolled boned pork loin**
2	**tablespoons dry mustard**
2	**teaspoons thyme**
½	**cup sherry**
½	**cup reduced-sodium soy sauce**

2	**garlic cloves, minced**
1	**teaspoon ginger powder, or 2 teaspoons grated gingerroot**

Currant Sauce

1	**(10-ounce) jar currant jelly**
2	**tablespoons sherry**

1	**tablespoon reduced-sodium soy sauce**

For the pork, rub the surface of the pork with a mixture of the dry mustard and thyme. Place the pork in a sealable plastic bag or dish. Pour a mixture of sherry, soy sauce, garlic and ginger powder over the pork and seal tightly. Marinate in the refrigerator for 3 to 10 hours, turning occasionally; drain.

Arrange the pork in a shallow roasting pan. Roast for 2½ hours or until a meat thermometer placed in the thickest portion of the pork registers 160 degrees. Remove from the oven. Let stand, covered with foil, at room temperature for 20 to 30 minutes. Slice and arrange on a serving platter.

For the sauce, combine the currant jelly, sherry and soy sauce in a saucepan. Cook until blended and heated through, stirring frequently. Drizzle the sauce over the sliced pork. *Yield: 16 servings.*

Approx Per Serving: Cal 292; Prot 32 g; Carbo 14 g; T Fat 11 g; 34% Calories from Fat; Chol 86 mg; Fiber <1 g; Sod 353 mg; Vit A 3 RE; Vit C 1 mg; Ca 27 mg; Iron 2 mg
Nutritional information includes the entire amount of marinade.

PULLED BARBECUED PORK

This barbecue sauce recipe is low in both oil and sugar, two ingredients that are concentrated in most barbecue sauces.

Pork
1   (4-pound) pork loin

Southwest Barbecue Sauce

2	tablespoons butter or margarine	1	tablespoon dry mustard
1	cup vinegar	2	tablespoons chili powder
1	cup water	1/8	teaspoon cayenne pepper
1/2	cup ketchup	1/2	teaspoon black pepper
2	tablespoons Worcestershire sauce	1	teaspoon salt
•	Juice of 1 lemon	1/4	cup packed brown sugar
		1	garlic clove, minced
		1	onion, grated

For the pork, arrange fat side up on a rack in a shallow roasting pan. Roast at 325 degrees for 30 to 35 minutes per pound or until a meat thermometer inserted in the thickest portion of the pork registers 160 degrees; do not insert the thermometer into fat or bone. Cool slightly. Discard the fat and shred the pork into a saucepan.

For the sauce, heat the butter in a saucepan until melted. Stir in the vinegar, water, ketchup, Worcestershire sauce, lemon juice, dry mustard, chili powder, cayenne pepper, black pepper, salt, brown sugar, garlic and onion in the order listed. Cook for 10 minutes, stirring frequently. Add to the pork and mix well. Cook just until heated through, stirring frequently. Serve on heated hamburger buns. *Yield: 16 servings.*

Approx Per Serving: Cal 225; Prot 25 g; Carbo 8 g; T Fat 10 g; 41% Calories from Fat; Chol 73 mg; Fiber 1 g; Sod 332 mg; Vit A 56 RE; Vit C 4 mg; Ca 29 mg; Iron 1 mg

Proteins supply amino acids. Amino acids are building blocks that build and repair body tissues. Protein is an energy source only if carbohydrates or fat are not available. Fat insulates the body, as well as protects and pads the organs. Fat adds flavor and aroma to food. Carbohydrates are the primary energy source for the body. They help to digest and regulate fat and to metabolize protein.

Chicken or VEAL MARSALA

8	ounces veal, thinly sliced	8	ounces fresh mushrooms, sliced
1/3	cup flour		
•	Salt and pepper to taste	1	cup dry marsala
1	tablespoon butter	1	cup beef broth
1	tablespoon olive oil or canola oil	1	tablespoon butter

Coat the veal with a mixture of the flour, salt and pepper. Heat 1 tablespoon butter and olive oil in a skillet over medium heat until hot. Add the veal. Sauté until the veal is light brown on both sides. Remove the veal to a platter with a slotted spoon, reserving the pan drippings.

Add the mushrooms, wine and ½ cup of the broth to the reserved pan drippings, stirring to incorporate any brown bits into the mixture. Bring to a boil, stirring frequently. Return the veal to the skillet; reduce heat.

Simmer, covered, for 20 to 25 minutes or until the sauce is of the desired consistency, stirring occasionally. Remove the veal to a heated serving platter with a slotted spoon, reserving the sauce.

Stir the remaining ½ cup broth into the sauce. Bring to a boil, stirring frequently. Boil until of a syrupy consistency, stirring frequently. Add 1 tablespoon butter and mix well. Drizzle over the veal. Spoon over hot cooked rice or pasta if desired. *Yield: 4 servings.*

Approx Per Serving: Cal 352; Prot 17 g; Carbo 17 g; T Fat 17 g; 43% Calories from Fat; Chol 68 mg; Fiber 1 g; Sod 295 mg; Vit A 53 RE; Vit C 1 mg; Ca 24 mg; Iron 1 mg

Brunswick Stew

A Virginia specialty, at one time prepared with squirrel or rabbit, Brunswick Stew is said to have originated in Brunswick County, Virginia. Today's version substitutes chicken. For many years, it has been the principal culinary attraction at political rallies, family reunions, tobacco gatherings, and other social events.

1	(4- to 5-pound) chicken or squirrel, cut into quarters	3	medium potatoes, sliced
1½	quarts water	⅛	teaspoon cayenne pepper
1	medium onion, sliced	•	Salt to taste
2	slices bacon, chopped	•	Chili sauce to taste
1	(16-ounce) can peeled tomatoes	•	Worcestershire sauce to taste
1	(10-ounce) package frozen whole kernel corn	•	Tabasco sauce to taste
1	(10-ounce) package frozen lima beans	½	cup fine bread crumbs

Combine the chicken, water, onion and bacon in a 6-quart heavy stockpot. Cook for 1 hour or until the chicken is almost cooked through. Cool slightly. Chop the chicken into bite-size pieces, discarding the skin and bones. Return the chicken to the saucepan. Stir in the undrained tomatoes, corn, lima beans, potatoes and cayenne pepper.

Cook until the vegetables are tender and the chicken is cooked through, stirring occasionally. Season with salt, chili sauce, Worcestershire sauce and Tabasco sauce. Stir in the bread crumbs just before serving. *Yield: 6 servings.*

Approx Per Serving: Cal 478; Prot 49 g; Carbo 43 g; T Fat 13 g; 24% Calories from Fat; Chol 121 mg; Fiber 6 g; Sod 398 mg; Vit A 67 RE; Vit C 34 mg; Ca 79 mg; Iron 4 mg

Cutting boards can harbor harmful bacteria. Acrylic, glass, marble, plastic, or wood? You choose, following these simple guidelines. Use two cutting boards in your kitchen, one strictly to cut raw meats, poultry, and seafood, and the other for ready-to-eat foods, such as breads, fruits, and vegetables. Wash cutting boards thoroughly in hot, soapy water after each use. Air dry or pat dry with fresh paper towels. Discard cutting boards with cracks, crevices, and excessive knife scars.

Substitute evaporated skim milk for heavy whipping cream to reduce the fat grams.

CHICKEN FLORENTINE

1	pound boneless skinless chicken breasts
1	tablespoon olive oil
1	teaspoon minced garlic
2	(10-ounce) packages frozen chopped spinach, thawed, drained
¼	teaspoon nutmeg
3	tablespoons flour
1	cup dry white wine
1	cup whipping cream
½	cup chicken broth
⅓	cup grated Parmesan cheese
•	Salt and pepper to taste
2	cups cooked rice or pasta

Cut the chicken into ½-inch strips. Heat a large skillet over medium-high heat. Add the olive oil and heat until hot. Add the chicken and garlic. Sauté until the chicken is brown on both sides.

Press the spinach to remove the excess moisture. Stir the spinach into skillet and add the nutmeg. Whisk the flour into the wine in a bowl until blended. Add the whipping cream, broth and cheese and stir well. Add to the chicken mixture and mix well.

Cook for 2 minutes or until thickened, stirring constantly. Season with salt and pepper. Spoon over the hot cooked rice on a serving platter. *Yield: 4 servings.*

Approx Per Serving: Cal 600; Prot 35 g; Carbo 36 g; T Fat 31 g; 47% Calories from Fat; Chol 151 mg; Fiber 5 g; Sod 438 mg; Vit A 1371 RE; Vit C 35 mg; Ca 337 mg; Iron 5 mg

CRISPY CHICKEN

2 ounces cornflakes, crushed	1/8 teaspoon pepper
1 tablespoon grated lemon zest	1 egg white
1 teaspoon dry mustard	2 teaspoons lemon juice
1/2 teaspoon garlic powder	4 (6-ounce) chicken breasts, skinned
1/4 teaspoon paprika	

Combine the cornflakes, lemon zest, dry mustard, garlic powder, paprika and pepper in a bowl and mix well. Combine the egg white and lemon juice in a small bowl and whisk lightly.

Dip the chicken in the egg mixture and coat with the crumb mixture. Arrange the chicken in a single layer in an ungreased baking pan. Bake at 350 degrees for 1 hour. *Yield: 4 servings.*

Approx Per Serving: Cal 244; Prot 36 g; Carbo 13 g; T Fat 4 g; 16% Calories from Fat; Chol 94 mg; Fiber 1 g; Sod 246 mg; Vit A 113 RE; Vit C 10 mg; Ca 21 mg; Iron 6 mg

Try this lower-fat alternative for fried chicken or fried fish. Dip skinless chicken or fish in egg whites and coat with seasoned bread crumbs. Arrange on a nonstick baking sheet sprayed with nonstick cooking spray. Bake at 350 degrees until cooked through. The result is fried chicken or fish minus the extra fat grams.

Virginia Barbecue Sauce

Combine 6 tablespoons cider vinegar, 3 tablespoons vegetable oil, 2 tablespoons Worcestershire sauce, 4 teaspoons lemon juice, 2 teaspoons salt, 4 to 6 drops of hot sauce and 1/2 teaspoon seasoned pepper (optional) in a saucepan. Simmer until heated through, stirring frequently. Use as a baste for grilling chicken, basting each time the chicken is turned on the grill. Yield: 3/4 cup.

French-Glazed Chicken

4	(4-ounce) boneless skinless chicken breasts	2	tablespoons water
1/4	cup reduced-calorie French salad dressing	1	tablespoon dried minced onion
2	tablespoons low-sugar apricot jam		

Arrange the chicken in a single layer in a 9x9-inch baking pan coated with nonstick cooking spray. Bake at 350 degrees for 20 minutes.

Combine the salad dressing, jam, water and minced onion in a bowl and mix well. Spoon over the chicken. Bake for 10 minutes longer or until the chicken is cooked through and hot. *Yield: 4 servings.*

Approx Per Serving: Cal 165; Prot 23 g; Carbo 9 g; T Fat 4 g; 21% Calories from Fat; Chol 63 mg; Fiber <1 g; Sod 185 mg; Vit A 26 RE; Vit C 5 mg; Ca 16 mg; Iron 1 mg

Honey Pecan Chicken

6   (6-ounce) boneless
    skinless chicken breasts
¼   cup honey
2   to 3 tablespoons frozen
    orange juice concentrate
1   (6-ounce) package chicken
    stove-top stuffing mix
    with seasoning packet

¼   cup (½ stick) margarine
1   cup boiling water
½   cup frozen orange juice
    concentrate
½   cup finely chopped pecans

Arrange the chicken in a single layer in a 9x13-inch baking pan. Combine the honey and 2 to 3 tablespoons orange juice concentrate in a bowl and mix well. Drizzle half the honey mixture over the chicken.

Combine the contents of the seasoning packet, margarine and boiling water in a bowl and stir until the margarine melts. Add the stuffing crumbs, ½ cup orange juice concentrate and pecans and stir just until moistened.

Press ½ cup of the stuffing mixture on top of each chicken breast. Drizzle with the remaining honey mixture. Bake at 375 degrees for 40 minutes or until cooked through. *Yield: 6 servings.*

Approx Per Serving: Cal 522; Prot 40 g; Carbo 46 g; T Fat 19 g; 33% Calories from Fat; Chol 94 mg; Fiber 2 g; Sod 618 mg; Vit A 92 RE; Vit C 45 mg; Ca 54 mg; Iron 3 mg

Make your own stuffing or dressing in order to reduce the sodium and fat content. Use a variety of breads—whole wheat, white, crackers, and/or corn bread. Add any variety of vegetables and/or dried fruits, such as celery, onions, apples, or dried apricots. For example, sauté 1 cup chopped onion and 1 cup chopped celery in a nonstick skillet sprayed with nonstick cooking spray until tender. Mix with 10 cups crumbled corn bread or biscuits. Stir in 1 cup nonfat chicken or turkey broth. Season with thyme, sage, parsley flakes, nutmeg, cloves, salt and pepper. Bake at 350 degrees for 25 minutes or until brown and bubbly.

Zesty Marinated Chicken

Go skinless on poultry before or after cooking. There is a layer of fat under the skin. By removing the skin, you can cut the fat content in half. For added flavor, cook poultry with the skin on to keep it tender and moist, but remove the skin before serving.

8 (6-ounce) boneless skinless chicken breasts
1 (16-ounce) bottle zesty Italian or Italian salad dressing
½ cup vermouth or white wine
¼ cup soy sauce
¼ cup packed brown sugar
2 tablespoons chopped fresh rosemary, or 2 teaspoons dried rosemary
1 teaspoon salt
1 teaspoon pepper

Arrange the chicken in a single layer in a dish. Combine the salad dressing, vermouth, soy sauce, brown sugar, rosemary, salt and pepper in a bowl and mix well. Pour over the chicken, turning to coat.

Marinate, covered, in the refrigerator for 8 hours or longer, turning occasionally; drain. Grill the chicken over hot coals until cooked through, turning occasionally. *Yield: 8 servings.*

Approx Per Serving: Cal 441; Prot 35 g; Carbo 12 g; T Fat 25 g; 52% Calories from Fat; Chol 94 mg; Fiber 0 g; Sod 2037 mg; Vit A 8 RE; Vit C <1 mg; Ca 31 mg; Iron 2 mg
Nutritional information includes the entire amount of marinade.

Chicken Stuffed with Spinach and Feta Cheese

Recipe furnished by Belle Kuisine of Richmond, Virginia.

10 (6-ounce) boneless skinless chicken breasts	1 ounce Parmesan cheese, grated
½ (10-ounce) package frozen chopped spinach, thawed, drained	2 eggs, beaten
	1 teaspoon oregano
1½ cups cottage cheese	½ teaspoon garlic powder
8 ounces feta cheese, crumbled	½ teaspoon pepper
	¼ teaspoon nutmeg
1¼ cups seasoned bread crumbs	6 tablespoons margarine, melted

Pound the chicken between sheets of waxed paper with a meat mallet until flattened. Press the spinach to remove the excess moisture.

Combine the spinach, cottage cheese, feta cheese, half the bread crumbs, Parmesan cheese, eggs, oregano, garlic powder, pepper and nutmeg in a bowl and mix well.

Spoon 3 ounces of the spinach mixture in the center of each chicken breast. Fold the chicken over to enclose the filling.

Arrange the chicken on a nonstick baking sheet. Brush with the margarine. Sprinkle with the remaining bread crumbs. Chill, covered, for 1 hour or longer. Bake at 325 degrees for 30 to 40 minutes or until the chicken is cooked through. *Yield: 10 servings.*

Approx Per Serving: Cal 422; Prot 46 g; Carbo 13 g; T Fat 19 g; 42% Calories from Fat; Chol 164 mg; Fiber 1 g; Sod 1016 mg; Vit A 253 RE; Vit C 4 mg; Ca 224 mg; Iron 2 mg

Sauté foods in a small amount of vegetable broth, defatted chicken or beef broth, or wine or juice instead of oil. Be careful not to use too much liquid or you will be boiling rather than sautéing and, as a result, will not achieve the same flavor. Steam or poach foods in flavorful, reduced-fat liquids.

Lower your dietary fat and cholesterol with these simple suggestions. Use skinless poultry and seafood in most of your main dishes. Use nonfat or reduced-fat cheeses and dried beans and peas. Select lean red meat no more than two to three times per week and prepare it without adding fat. Choose select and choice grades: top round, eye of round, pork tenderloin venison, and extra-lean ground beef. When browning meats, drain the fat before continuing to cook in the pan. Make soups and stews the day before serving. Chill and skim the fat off the top.

ROSEMARY AND
BRIE CHICKEN CRESCENTS

1	(8-count) can crescent rolls	1	egg, beaten
1½	cups chopped cooked chicken breasts	1	teaspoon rosemary, crushed
6	ounces Brie cheese or Swiss cheese, cubed	1	tablespoon grated Parmesan cheese
2	tablespoons finely chopped green onions		

Unroll the crescent roll dough. Separate into 4 rectangles, pressing the perforations to seal. Mix the chicken, Brie and green onions in a bowl.

Spoon ¼ of the chicken mixture in the center of each rectangle. Fold the short sides over the chicken mixture, overlapping slightly. Fold the remaining sides over about ½ inch to form a rectangle. Press the edges to seal. Arrange the rectangles seam side down in an ungreased 10x15-inch baking pan.

Make three 1-inch vents in the top of each rectangle. Brush with the egg and sprinkle with the rosemary and Parmesan cheese. Bake at 350 degrees for 20 to 22 minutes or until golden brown. Garnish with tomato slices, green onions and/or sprigs of fresh rosemary. *Yield: 4 servings.*

Approx Per Serving: Cal 477; Prot 30 g; Carbo 23 g; T Fat 29 g; 55% Calories from Fat; Chol 141 mg; Fiber 1 g; Sod 783 mg; Vit A 119 RE; Vit C 1 mg; Ca 128 mg; Iron 2 mg

ORANGE BOURBON TURKEY

1	(10- to 12-pound) fresh or thawed frozen turkey	⅓	cup molasses
2	cups fresh orange juice (about 6 oranges)	½	teaspoon salt
		4	oranges, peeled
1	cup water	¼	cup bourbon
½	cup bourbon	3	tablespoons flour
		¼	teaspoon salt

Remove the giblets and neck from the turkey and discard. Rinse the turkey with cold water and pat dry. Place the turkey in a large roasting bag. Pour a mixture of the orange juice, water, ½ cup bourbon and molasses over the turkey and seal tightly. Marinate in the refrigerator for 4 to 24 hours, turning occasionally. Drain, reserving the marinade.

Tie the turkey legs together with kitchen twine and tuck the wing tips under the turkey. Sprinkle ½ teaspoon salt in the inside cavity. Stuff the cavity with the oranges. Place the turkey on a broiler rack sprayed with nonstick cooking spray. Place in a broiler pan.

Bake at 350 degrees for 3 hours or until a meat thermometer registers 180 degrees. Cover the turkey loosely with foil if needed during the end of the roasting process to prevent overbrowning. Remove the turkey from the oven. Let stand, loosely covered with foil, for 10 minutes before serving. Discard the oranges.

Bring the reserved marinade to a boil in a saucepan over high heat; skim the foam. Reduce the heat to medium. Cook for 15 minutes or until reduced to 3½ cups, stirring occasionally. Whisk ¼ cup bourbon and flour in a bowl until blended. Stir into the marinade. Bring to a boil, stirring constantly. Boil for 1 minute, stirring constantly. Stir in ¼ teaspoon salt.

Arrange the turkey on a serving platter. Garnish with orange slices and sprigs of fresh parsley. Serve with the warm bourbon sauce.
Yield: 15 servings.

Approx Per Serving: Cal 393; Prot 54 g; Carbo 14 g; T Fat 9 g; 21% Calories from Fat; Chol 137 mg; Fiber 1 g; Sod 246 mg; Vit A 14 RE; Vit C 35 mg; Ca 78 mg; Iron 4 mg
Nutritional information includes the entire amount of marinade.

Do Thanksgiving festivities sometimes leave you feeling stuffed and guilty from overeating? Try eating a reduced-fat and reduced-calorie diet in the days preceding and following Thanksgiving in order to fit a more liberal Thanksgiving feast into your lifestyle. If you are cooking, offer reduced-fat alternatives to the higher-fat favorites like sausage stuffing or pumpkin pie. If you are not the cook, then offer to bring substitutes, such as apple dressing or a reduced-fat pumpkin pie. Suggest a half-time walk to get your guests out and moving. Avoid turkeys that have been injected with fat or butter. Cook the bird with the skin, but remove before serving your family and guests.

Turkey Cutlets in Apricot Sauce

1	cup apricot nectar	¹⁄₂	teaspoon pepper
1	teaspoon minced gingerroot	¹⁄₄	teaspoon salt
1	teaspoon soy sauce	1	teaspoon margarine
1	teaspoon cornstarch	4	green onions with tops, cut into 1-inch pieces
4	(4-ounce) turkey cutlets		

Combine the apricot nectar, gingerroot, soy sauce and cornstarch in a bowl and mix well. Sprinkle the cutlets with the pepper and salt. Heat the margarine in a 12-inch nonstick skillet over medium-high heat until melted.

Add the cutlets to the skillet. Sauté for 2 minutes; turn. Sauté for 1¹⁄₂ to 2 minutes longer or until cooked through. Remove to a platter with a slotted spoon, reserving the pan drippings. Cover to keep warm.

Stir the green onions into the reserved pan drippings. Cook for 30 seconds, stirring frequently. Stir in the apricot nectar mixture. Cook for 1 minute or until thickened, stirring constantly. Drizzle over the cutlets. *Yield: 4 servings.*

Approx Per Serving: Cal 184; Prot 30 g; Carbo 11 g; T Fat 2 g; 9% Calories from Fat; Chol 82 mg; Fiber 1 g; Sod 321 mg; Vit A 97 RE; Vit C 3 mg; Ca 26 mg; Iron 2 mg

Turkey and Beans

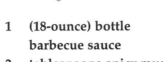

1½	pounds ground turkey	1	(18-ounce) bottle barbecue sauce
½	green bell pepper, chopped	2	tablespoons spicy mustard
1	small onion, chopped	2	(28-ounce) cans baked beans with brown sugar
1	tablespoon canola oil		

Brown the ground turkey with the bell pepper and onion in the canola oil in a skillet, stirring until the ground turkey is crumbly; drain. Stir in the barbecue sauce, mustard and beans.

Simmer for 30 minutes, stirring occasionally. You may substitute ground beef for the ground turkey. For variety, vary the flavors of barbecue sauce. *Yield: 8 servings.*

Approx Per Serving: Cal 429; Prot 29 g; Carbo 56 g; T Fat 14 g; 27% Calories from Fat; Chol 65 mg; Fiber 10 g; Sod 1423 mg; Vit A 60 RE; Vit C 15 mg; Ca 154 mg; Iron 5 mg

Do not assume poultry products are low in fat. Read the label; they may be high in both fat and sodium.

For safety's sake, do not thaw frozen turkeys at room temperature. Thaw in the refrigerator in the original wrapper on a tray for one to three days. When the wrapper is removed, thaw eighteen hours to two days in the refrigerator. You may thaw the bird immersed in cold water for three to four hours for a five- to eight-pound turkey or six to seven hours for larger birds, changing the water every thirty minutes.

Turkey Chili with White Beans

2	medium onions, chopped	½	teaspoon salt (optional)
2	carrots, peeled, chopped	¼	teaspoon cinnamon
2	ribs celery, chopped	2	bay leaves
2	teaspoons vegetable oil	1	(28-ounce) can whole tomatoes
1½	teaspoons oregano		
1½	teaspoons cumin	3	cups beef stock or broth
1½	pounds lean ground turkey	1	(8-ounce) can tomato sauce
		3	(15-ounce) cans white or kidney beans, drained, rinsed
1	tablespoon chili powder, or to taste		
1	tablespoon baking cocoa	2	cups rice or orzo, cooked

Sauté the onions, carrots and celery in the oil in a large saucepan over medium heat for 10 minutes or until the vegetables are light brown and tender. Stir in the oregano and cumin. Increase the heat to high. Add the ground turkey.

Cook until the turkey is brown and crumbly, stirring constantly. Stir in the chili powder, baking cocoa, salt, cinnamon and bay leaves. Add the undrained tomatoes, breaking the tomatoes into smaller pieces with the back of a spoon. Stir in the stock and tomato sauce. Bring to a boil; reduce heat.

Simmer for 45 minutes, stirring occasionally. Add the beans and mix well. Simmer for 10 minutes longer, stirring occasionally. Discard the bay leaves. Ladle over hot cooked rice or orzo in chili bowls. May serve with shredded cheese, additional chopped onion, chopped fresh cilantro, plain yogurt and/or reduced-fat sour cream. *Yield: 16 (1-cup) servings.*

Approx Per Serving: Cal 257; Prot 16 g; Carbo 37 g; T Fat 6 g; 19% Calories from Fat; Chol 33 mg; Fiber 5 g; Sod 639 mg; Vit A 314 RE; Vit C 12 mg; Ca 63 mg; Iron 3 mg

CREOLE COD

1 (1½-pound) codfish fillet
1 tablespoon margarine, softened
1 tablespoon flour
1 onion, thinly sliced
1 (16-ounce) can diced tomatoes
¼ cup chopped green bell pepper
• Salt and pepper to taste
1 bay leaf, crumbled

Cut the codfish into 6 equal portions. Coat each portion with the margarine and sprinkle with the flour. Arrange the codfish in a single layer in a baking dish coated with nonstick cooking spray.

Layer the onion, undrained tomatoes and bell pepper over the codfish. Sprinkle with salt, pepper and the bay leaf. Bake at 350 degrees for 30 minutes or until the codfish flakes easily. Garnish with sprigs of fresh parsley. *Yield: 6 servings.*

Approx Per Serving: Cal 102; Prot 13 g; Carbo 6 g; T Fat 2 g; 22% Calories from Fat; Chol 30 mg; Fiber 1 g; Sod 194 mg; Vit A 61 RE; Vit C 16 mg; Ca 25 mg; Iron 1 mg

Fish has fewer calories than meat and is lower in fat and extremely nutritious. An average serving, approximately 4 ounces, supplies one-third to one-half of the daily protein requirements, as well as B vitamins, thiamin, riboflavin, and niacin. Fish is also a source of iodine, copper, and iron and, if cooked with the dissolved bones, calcium and phosphorus.

Brine is a solution of salt and water, preferably soft water. Its purpose is to draw the natural sugars and moisture from foods and form lactic acids, which protect the foods against spoilage from bacteria. A 10-percent brine, about the strongest used in food processing, is made by dissolving one and one-half cups of salt in one gallon of liquid, or six tablespoons of salt to each quart of liquid. But after brining, as more liquid continues to be drawn from the fruits and vegetables, the brine may be weakened. Always allow about two gallons of 10-percent brine plus enough food to fill a four-gallon jar. A rule of thumb to test for 10-percent brine is that it will float a two-ounce egg so the shell just breaks the surface of the liquid.

Halibut Kabobs

2	pounds halibut steaks, skinned, boned	1	tablespoon grated lemon zest
½	cup (1 stick) margarine, melted	1	garlic clove, minced
¼	cup white wine	•	Salt and pepper to taste
2	tablespoons lemon juice	24	cherry tomatoes
2	tablespoons minced fresh parsley	2	large green bell peppers, cut into chunks

Cut the halibut into 1½-inch cubes. Combine the margarine, white wine, lemon juice, parsley, lemon zest, garlic, salt and pepper in a bowl and mix well. Add the halibut and toss to coat. Marinate at room temperature for 30 minutes, stirring occasionally.

Drain, reserving the marinade. Thread the halibut on skewers, adding the cherry tomatoes and bell peppers at desired intervals.

Grill the kabobs 8 inches from the heat source for 10 minutes or until the fish flakes easily, turning and basting with the reserved marinade frequently. Serve over wild rice. *Yield: 6 servings.*

Approx Per Serving: Cal 427; Prot 21 g; Carbo 7 g; T Fat 34 g; 72% Calories from Fat; Chol 63 mg; Fiber 2 g; Sod 296 mg; Vit A 249 RE; Vit C 63 mg; Ca 23 mg; Iron 2 mg
Nutritional information includes the entire amount of marinade.

CRAB CAKES

2	slices bread	¼	teaspoon dry mustard
1	egg, lightly beaten	⅛	teaspoon ginger
1	tablespoon mayonnaise	⅛	teaspoon pepper
1	tablespoon Worcestershire sauce	1	pound crab meat, flaked
1	tablespoon baking powder	2	to 3 tablespoons vegetable oil
1	teaspoon parsley flakes		

Crumble the bread finely into a bowl. Stir in the egg. Add the mayonnaise, Worcestershire sauce, baking powder, parsley flakes, dry mustard, ginger and pepper and mix well. Add the crab meat and mix gently.

Shape the crab meat mixture into 8 cakes. Brown the crab cakes in the oil in a skillet over medium heat until brown on both sides; drain. *Yield: 8 crab cakes.*

Approx Per Crab Cake: Cal 151; Prot 13 g; Carb 6 g; T Fat 8 g; 49% Calories from Fat; Chol 68 mg; Fiber <1 g; Sod 461 mg; Vit A 29 RE; Vit C 2 mg; Ca 146 mg; Iron 1 mg

Old Receipt for Salt Herring

Take fresh herring, remove the head and insides and split the fish so that it can lie flat. Use as little water as possible in rinsing the fish. Pack herring in a wooden or earthen crock, a layer of fish and a layer of coarse salt. Have the last layer one of salt and put a large plate, with a rock on top, so that all the fish will be in the cure. So prepared they will keep indefinitely. When you are ready to use the fish, soak them at least twenty-four hours in cold water, changing the water several times. Salt herring may be fried, but is best broiled with lots of butter.

Substituting nonfat cheeses for higher-fat cheeses in many casseroles may not always be successful, as nonfat cheeses do not melt in the same manner as traditional cheeses. If you choose to use nonfat cheese, shred it and sprinkle on the top of the casserole several minutes before the end of the baking process. Or use the higher-fat cheeses and cut the amount used in half.

CRAB FLORENTINE

6 tablespoons butter	²/₃ cup white wine
¼ cup flour	½ cup cheese crackers,
1¹/₃ cups milk	crumbled
2 chicken bouillon cubes	2 tablespoons butter, melted
1 cup shredded Cheddar cheese	2 (10-ounce) packages frozen chopped spinach, cooked,
7 ounces crab meat, rinsed, drained, flaked	drained

Heat 6 tablespoons butter in a skillet until melted. Add the flour, stirring until blended. Stir in the milk and bouillon cubes. Cook until thickened, stirring constantly. Stir in the cheese, crab meat and white wine.

Toss the cracker crumbs and 2 tablespoons butter in a bowl until coated. Spread equal portions of the spinach in each of 8 individual baking shells. Spoon the crab meat mixture over the spinach. Sprinkle with the cracker crumbs. Bake at 425 degrees for 15 to 20 minutes or until bubbly. *Yield: 8 servings.*

Approx Per Serving: Cal 275; Prot 13 g; Carbo 11 g; T Fat 19 g; 61% Calories from Fat; Chol 70 mg; Fiber 2 g; Sod 692 mg; Vit A 719 RE; Vit C 18 mg; Ca 257 mg; Iron 2 mg

CRAB IMPERIAL

3 tablespoons reduced-fat mayonnaise	• Thyme to taste
2 tablespoons prepared mustard	• Basil to taste
2 eggs, beaten	2 tablespoons Worcestershire sauce
¼ teaspoon salt	1 pound crab meat, flaked
¼ teaspoon pepper	1 slice bread, crumbled

Combine the mayonnaise, prepared mustard, eggs, salt, pepper, thyme, basil and Worcestershire sauce in a bowl and mix well. Add the crab meat and bread crumbs and mix gently.

Spoon the crab meat mixture into a baking dish. Bake at 350 degrees for 35 minutes or until brown and bubbly. *Yield: 4 servings.*

Approx Per Serving: Cal 214; Prot 28 g; Carbo 9 g; T Fat 7 g; 29% Calories from Fat; Chol 189 mg; Fiber <1 g; Sod 853 mg; Vit A 81 RE; Vit C 5 mg; Ca 98 mg; Iron 2 mg

Baked White Fish

Season four 3- to 4-ounce white fish fillets with white pepper, garlic powder, dillweed, paprika and parsley flakes. Arrange on a baking sheet sprayed with nonstick cooking spray. Drizzle each fillet with 2 tablespoons of wine and fresh lemon juice. Bake in a 325-degree oven for 20 minutes or until the fish flakes easily.

CRAB NEWBURG

2 cups water	8 ounces crab meat, rinsed, drained, flaked
1 cup long grain rice	
2 tablespoons butter	2 tablespoons dry white wine
3 tablespoons flour	
2 tablespoons dry sherry	2 tablespoons lemon juice
1½ cups 1% milk	¼ teaspoon salt
1 medium egg yolk	¼ teaspoon paprika

Bring the water to a boil in a saucepan over high heat. Stir in the rice. Return to a boil; reduce heat. Cook, covered, for 25 minutes.

Heat the butter in a saucepan over low heat until melted. Add the flour and stir until blended. Whisk in the sherry and 1% milk. Cook over medium heat for 10 minutes or until thickened and of a sauce consistency, whisking frequently.

Whisk the egg yolk in a bowl. Stir a small amount of the hot sauce into the egg yolk. Stir the egg yolk into the hot mixture. Cook until thickened, stirring constantly. Stir in the crab meat, white wine, lemon juice, salt and paprika. Cook for 3 to 4 minutes or until heated through, stirring frequently. Serve over the hot cooked rice. Garnish with lemon wedges. *Yield: 4 servings.*

Approx Per Serving: Cal 364; Prot 19 g; Carbo 47 g; T Fat 9 g; 23% Calories from Fat; Chol 112 mg; Fiber 1 g; Sod 455 mg; Vit A 148 RE; Vit C 6 mg; Ca 167 mg; Iron 3 mg

SHRIMP SCAMPI

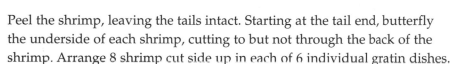

2	pounds large shrimp (about 48 shrimp)	¼	cup fresh lemon juice
1	cup chopped red bell pepper	½	teaspoon salt
		¼	teaspoon pepper
8	garlic cloves, crushed	•	Paprika to taste
3	tablespoons margarine	6	cups hot cooked angel hair pasta (about 12 ounces uncooked pasta)
½	cup dry white wine		
¼	cup minced fresh parsley		

Peel the shrimp, leaving the tails intact. Starting at the tail end, butterfly the underside of each shrimp, cutting to but not through the back of the shrimp. Arrange 8 shrimp cut side up in each of 6 individual gratin dishes.

Sauté the bell pepper and garlic in the margarine in a skillet for 2 minutes. Remove from heat. Stir in the white wine, parsley, lemon juice, salt and pepper. Spoon over the shrimp. Sprinkle with paprika.

Broil for 6 minutes or until the shrimp are cooked through. Serve with the hot cooked pasta. *Yield: 6 servings.*

Approx Per Serving: Cal 387; Prot 30 g; Carbo 44 g; T Fat 8 g; 19% Calories from Fat; Chol 215 mg; Fiber 3 g; Sod 513 mg; Vit A 284 RE; Vit C 59 mg; Ca 70 mg; Iron 6 mg

To lower the amount of fat in your own recipes, spray a nonstick skillet with nonstick cooking spray. Reduce the amount of oil, butter, or margarine required for sautéing meats and vegetables by half.

Shrimp and Spinach with Walnut Topping

1	pound large shrimp, peeled, butterflied	1	teaspoon roasted sesame oil
1½	tablespoons dry sherry	¼	teaspoon ground red chile pepper
1	tablespoon grated gingerroot	2	to 3 tablespoons chopped walnuts
⅓	cup chicken or vegetable broth	1	teaspoon peanut oil
2	tablespoons soy sauce	10	ounces fresh spinach, trimmed
2	tablespoons ketchup	1	tablespoon minced garlic
1½	tablespoons sherry	1	red bell pepper, julienned
1	tablespoon cornstarch	2	to 3 tablespoons water
1	tablespoon rice wine or cider vinegar	4	to 6 scallions, cut into ½-inch slices
2	teaspoons brown sugar		

Combine the shrimp, 1½ tablespoons sherry and gingerroot in a bowl and mix well. Marinate in the refrigerator for 30 to 45 minutes, stirring occasionally. Combine the broth, soy sauce, ketchup, 1½ tablespoons sherry, cornstarch, rice wine vinegar, brown sugar, sesame oil and chile pepper in a bowl, mix well and set aside.

Spray a wok with nonstick cooking spray. Heat over high heat for 3 to 5 minutes; do not allow to smoke. Add the walnuts. Stir-fry for 30 seconds. Remove to a bowl. Drizzle the peanut oil in the wok, turning to coat the sides. Add the spinach. Stir-fry for 2 minutes. Remove to a serving platter. Cover to keep warm. Add the garlic, bell pepper and water to the wok. Stir-fry for 2 minutes. Add the undrained shrimp and scallions.

Stir-fry for 3 to 4 minutes or until the shrimp turn pink. Stir in the broth mixture. Cook for 2 to 3 minutes, stirring constantly. Spoon over the spinach. Sprinkle with the walnuts. You may serve over hot cooked rice. *Yield: 4 servings.*

Approx Per Serving: Cal 218; Prot 22 g; Carbo 16 g; T Fat 7 g; 29% Calories from Fat; Chol 161 mg; Fiber 3 g; Sod 1062 mg; Vit A 716 RE; Vit C 83 mg; Ca 132 mg; Iron 5 mg

Monticello

Charlottesville Harvest

An Old Receipt for Pease with Mint

"Shell your pease just before you want them, put them into a very small quantity of boiling water, with a little salt and a lump of loaf sugar, when they begin to dent in the middle they are enough, strain them in a sieve, put a good lump of butter into a mug or small dish, give your pease a shake up with the butter, put them on a dish, and send them to table. Boil a sprig of mint in another water, chop it fine and lay it in lumps round the edge of your dish."

The Art of Cookery Made Plain and Easy, 1789
Hannah Glasse

Thomas Jefferson was famous for his dedication to gastronomy.
While serving as Secretary of State and then as Vice-President, this epicurean enjoyed numerous dinners and levees featuring the great variety of foods offered at the Philadelphia markets. Of all the kinds of vegetables, peas always remained his favorite.

Fruits and Vegetables of Virginia

The settlers quickly accepted and adopted the Indians' chief dietary staple—maize, which gave them two crops in one season. Corn was often used as "roasting ears." Green corn appeared in stew-like mixtures throughout the season. Indians dried corn in hot ashes; they boiled dried corn with beans, meat, and fish in the winter. To make hominy, the Indians soaked the dried corn, then pounded it. They boiled it for twelve hours. Other native foods were yams, beans, peas, squash, melons, and pumpkins, as well as deer, turkey, and wild game.

Dr. Neige Todhunter wrote in "Seven Centuries of Cookbooks—Treasures and Pleasures" that succotash was an early American dish. The colonists learned to cook this dish from the Indians when they cooked corn and beans with fat meat. The Indians named it "m'sick-quo-tash" or "sukqutachhash," which was named succotash by the English colonists.

Around 1620, the Virginians boasted of their gardens, which were planted near the kitchen door. They enjoyed good supplies of peas, beans, turnips, radishes, parsley, onions, potatoes, cabbage, cauliflower, pumpkins, carrots, parsnips, thyme, savory, and lettuce. Also, Virginians were blessed with four seasons, which provided them with a variety of fresh fruits in addition to the vegetables.

Dr. Maryellen Spencer wrote that the early colonists loved fruit orchards and cultivated them with great pride. Among the most popular fruits were apples, pears, peaches, quinces, and apricots. Some varieties of grapes, plums, cherries, and mulberries grew wild.

The following note was written March 1, 1812, by Thomas Jefferson to one of his overseers . . . "I inclose some lettuce seed, and shall be glad if you will sow about 8 or 10 feet of one of the beds behing the stable, and do the same on the lst. day of every month till the fall. . . ."

Anise-Marinated Fruit

2	tablespoons anise seeds	1	orange, peeled, sliced, cut into quarters
1	cup water	1	nectarine, cut into thin wedges
¾	cup sugar	1	plum, cut into thin wedges
1	tablespoon lemon juice	½	cup seedless red or green grapes
½	small pineapple, cut into bite-size pieces	½	lime, sliced
½	small honeydew melon, cut into bite-size pieces		
½	small cantaloupe, cut into bite-size pieces		

Tie the anise seeds in several layers of cheesecloth. Combine the water, sugar and lemon juice in a saucepan and mix well. Add the cheesecloth bag. Bring to a boil. Boil until the sugar dissolves, stirring frequently; reduce heat. Cook over medium heat for 5 to 7 minutes or until golden brown in color and of the consistency of a thin syrup, stirring frequently. Let stand until cool.

Combine the pineapple, honeydew melon, cantaloupe, orange, nectarine, plum, grapes and lime in a bowl and toss gently. Add the syrup and cheesecloth bag and mix until coated. Marinate, covered, in the refrigerator for 2 to 10 hours, stirring occasionally. Discard the cheesecloth bag. Spoon the fruit mixture onto lettuce-lined salad plates.
Yield: 10 servings.

Approx Per Serving: Cal 121; Prot 1 g; Carbo 30 g; T Fat <1 g; 3% Calories from Fat; Chol 0 mg; Fiber 2 g; Sod 18 mg; Vit A 95 RE; Vit C 31 mg; Ca 21 mg; Iron 1 mg

Experience is the best teacher in choosing quality fruits, but here are a few pointers on buying certain types of fruits. Select plump, solid berries with good color. Avoid stained containers, indicating wet or leaky berries. Berries such as blackberries and raspberries with clinging caps may be underripe. Strawberries without caps may be too ripe. With cantaloupes, thick close netting on the rind indicates the best quality. Cantaloupes are ripe when the stem scar is smooth and space between the netting is yellow or yellow-green. They are best when fully ripe with a fruity odor. Honeydew melons are ripe when the rind is a creamy to yellowish color and has a velvety texture. Immature honeydew melons are whitish-green. Ripe watermelons have some yellow color on one side. If melons are white or pale green on one side, they are not ripe.

Spiced Peaches

If your local grocery store does not stock Spiced Peaches, try this easy recipe. Bring 3 to 4 pounds sugar, 2 cups cider vinegar, 3 cinnamon sticks and 36 whole cloves to a boil in a large stockpot. Cook until the sugar dissolves. Add 7 pounds of peeled peaches in very small batches to the syrup, cooking the peaches until they can be pierced easily with a wooden pick. Remove the peaches 1 at a time as they become tender. Cook the syrup for 1 hour longer or until thickened, stirring occasionally. Pour over the peaches. Let stand at room temperature for 8 to 10 hours. Pack the peaches into hot sterilized jars. Ladle the syrup over the peaches, leaving ½ inch headspace; seal with 2-piece lids. To store, process in a boiling water bath for 15 minutes.

SPICED PEACH SALAD

1	(29-ounce) can spiced peaches (see sidebar)	1	(3-ounce) package lemon gelatin
1	(16-ounce) can white grapes or Queen Anne cherries	1	(3-ounce) package orange gelatin
¾	cup orange juice	½	cup ginger preserves
		½	cup pecan pieces

Drain the peaches and grapes, reserving the juice. Slice the peaches and grapes. Combine the reserved juices with enough of the orange juice to measure 4 cups and pour into a saucepan.

Heat the juices until hot. Remove from heat. Combine the hot juices, lemon gelatin and orange gelatin in a heatproof bowl, stirring until dissolved. Chill until partially set. Stir in the peaches, grapes, preserves and pecans. Spoon into a 9x13-inch dish. Chill until set. Serve on lettuce-lined salad plates. *Yield: 12 servings.*

Approx Per Serving: Cal 203; Prot 2 g; Carbo 45 g; T Fat 4 g; 14% Calories from Fat; Chol 0 mg; Fiber 2 g; Sod 50 mg; Vit A 28 RE; Vit C 13 mg; Ca 14 mg; Iron 1 mg

Sunshine Fruit Salad

4   (11-ounce) cans mandarin
    oranges
1   (15-ounce) can pineapple
    tidbits
1   cup orange juice
2   (4-ounce) packages
    vanilla cook-and-serve
    pudding mix

2   (3-ounce) packages
    tapioca cook-and-serve
    pudding mix
1   small bunch white grapes
6   strawberries (optional)

Drain the mandarin oranges and pineapple, reserving the juices. Combine the reserved juices and orange juice with enough water to measure 6 cups. Combine the pudding mixes in a saucepan and mix well. Stir in the fruit juice mixture. Bring the pudding mixture to a boil, stirring constantly. Let stand until cool.

Fold the mandarin oranges, pineapple and grapes into the pudding mixture. Spoon into a serving bowl. Chill, covered, until serving time. Arrange the strawberries in a decorative pattern over the salad. You may substitute your favorite fruit for the grapes. *Yield: 12 servings.*

Approx Per Serving: Cal 221; Prot 1 g; Carbo 57 g; T Fat <1 g; 1% Calories from Fat; Chol 0 mg; Fiber 1 g; Sod 191 mg; Vit A 93 RE; Vit C 35 mg; Ca 19 mg; Iron 1 mg

While serving in France in the mid-1780s, Thomas Jefferson traveled extensively in Europe and always showed the keenest interest in food. On his return to Virginia, he introduced southern and American eaters to vanilla extract, olives and olive oil, wines from France, pasta from Italy, waffles from Holland, and recipes for ice cream, meringues, and oil and vinegar salad dressings. His extensive vegetable plot was an experimental farm where new varieties of plants were grown.

Oriental Chicken Salad

½	head cabbage, finely shredded	2	tablespoons slivered almonds, toasted
1	(3-ounce) package ramen noodles without seasoning packet, broken	2	green onions, chopped
		½	cup vegetable oil
2	(6-ounce) boneless skinless chicken breasts, cooked, chopped	3	tablespoons vinegar
		2	tablespoons sugar
		1	teaspoon salt
2	tablespoons sesame seeds, toasted	1	teaspoon MSG
		½	teaspoon pepper

Toss the cabbage, ramen noodles, chicken, sesame seeds, almonds and green onions in a bowl.

Whisk the oil, vinegar, sugar, salt, MSG and pepper in a bowl. Add to the cabbage mixture and toss to coat. Chill, covered, until serving time. *Yield: 6 servings.*

Approx Per Serving: Cal 359; Prot 15 g; Carbo 19 g; T Fat 26 g; 63% Calories from Fat; Chol 31 mg; Fiber 2 g; Sod 560 mg; Vit A 14 RE; Vit C 25 mg; Ca 56 mg; Iron 1 mg

Black Bean, Corn and Bell Pepper Salad

2   (15-ounce) cans black beans, drained, rinsed
2   cups chopped fresh tomatoes
1   green bell pepper, chopped
1   red bell pepper, chopped
1   cup chopped red onion
1   cup cooked fresh or thawed frozen whole kernel corn
2   tablespoons wine vinegar

2   tablespoons fresh lime juice
1   tablespoon grated lime zest (optional)
2   teaspoons cumin
1½ teaspoons olive oil
2   garlic cloves, minced
¼   teaspoon red pepper flakes, crushed
½   cup chopped fresh cilantro
•   Salt and pepper to taste

Combine the black beans, tomatoes, bell peppers, onion and corn in a bowl and mix well. Whisk the wine vinegar, lime juice, lime zest, cumin, olive oil, garlic and red pepper flakes in a bowl.

Pour the dressing over the bean mixture and toss to coat. Fold in the cilantro. Season with salt and pepper. Let stand for 1 hour before serving. Serve at room temperature or chilled. You may substitute 2 cups cooked dried black beans for the canned black beans. *Yield: 6 servings.*

Approx Per Serving: Cal 187; Prot 10 g; Carbo 34 g; T Fat 3 g; 13% Calories from Fat; Chol 0 mg; Fiber 10 g; Sod 449 mg; Vit A 173 RE; Vit C 72 mg; Ca 60 mg; Iron 4 mg

Tomatoes are an excellent source of lycopene. It has been reported that lycopene may help reduce the risk of cancer and help protect against heart disease.

Make your own frozen juice pops in an ice cube tray, or freeze grapes, straw-berries, or chunks of bananas, pineapple, or melons.

FRESH BROCCOLI SALAD

- **Florets of 2 bunches broccoli**
- 1 **bunch green onions, sliced**
- ½ **cup golden raisins**
- 6 **slices crisp-cooked bacon, drained, crumbled**

- 1 **cup nonfat mayonnaise**
- 1 **tablespoon vinegar**
- 1 **tablespoon sugar**

Toss the broccoli, green onions, raisins and bacon in a bowl. Combine the mayonnaise, vinegar and sugar in a bowl and mix well. Add to the broccoli mixture and mix gently until coated. Chill, covered, for several hours before serving. *Yield: 8 servings.*

Approx Per Serving: Cal 90; Prot 3 g; Carbo 15 g; T Fat 3 g; 30% Calories from Fat; Chol 4 mg; Fiber 1 g; Sod 294 mg; Vit A 59 RE; Vit C 19 mg; Ca 23 mg; Iron 1 mg

CONFETTI COLESLAW

The use of yogurt in the dressing provides a valuable source of calcium, a nutrient limited in many diets. If time is of the essence, substitute prepared coleslaw mix for the cabbage mixture.

Creamy Coleslaw Dressing

³⁄₄ cup nonfat yogurt, nonfat mayonnaise or soft tofu	2 teaspoons sugar or honey
¹⁄₂ cup cider vinegar	1 teaspoon prepared horseradish (optional)
¹⁄₄ cup nonfat sour cream (optional)	¹⁄₂ teaspoon celery seeds (optional)
1 tablespoon Dijon mustard	

Slaw

8 cups finely sliced green cabbage	¹⁄₂ cup julienned red or green bell pepper
1 cup grated carrots	• Salt and pepper to taste
1 cup chopped red onion	

For the dressing, whisk the yogurt, cider vinegar, sour cream, Dijon mustard, sugar, horseradish and celery seeds in a bowl until mixed. Use a combination of the yogurt, mayonnaise and tofu or use individually for variety.

For the slaw, combine the cabbage, carrots, onion and bell pepper in a bowl and mix well. Add the dressing and toss to coat. Season with salt and pepper. Chill, covered, for 1 hour before serving. *Yield: 8 (1-cup) servings.*

Approx Per Serving: Cal 50; Prot 2 g; Carbo 11 g; T Fat <1 g; 7% Calories from Fat; Chol <1 mg; Fiber 3 g; Sod 78 mg; Vit A 429 RE; Vit C 36 mg; Ca 73 mg; Iron 1 mg

Substitute a mixture of plain nonfat yogurt and sugar to taste for commercially prepared slaw dressing. This is a bonus for adding calcium and lowering fat content.

Herbed Yogurt Dressing

Combine 1 cup plain yogurt and 1 tablespoon lemon juice. Season with any of the following herbs: chopped fresh chives, parsley, oregano, dill-weed, sage, rosemary, thyme, and/or paprika. Yield: 1 cup.

DUTCH SALAD

2	heads cauliflower, cut into bite-size pieces	6	ounces bacon bits
2	bunches green onions, chopped	8	ounces sliced almonds, toasted
2	cups shredded sharp Cheddar cheese	1	cup sugar
		¾	cup lemon juice
		2	cups mayonnaise

Layer the cauliflower, green onions, cheese, bacon bits and almonds in the order listed in a salad bowl.

Combine the sugar and lemon juice in a bowl and mix well. Stir in the mayonnaise. Pour over the layered ingredients; do not stir. Run a sharp knife around the edge of the bowl to allow the dressing mixture to penetrate the salad.

Marinate, covered, in the refrigerator for 4 to 10 hours. The flavor is enhanced the longer the marinating time. You may substitute nonfat Cheddar cheese for the Cheddar cheese and nonfat plain yogurt for the mayonnaise. *Yield: 15 (½-cup) servings.*

Approx Per Serving: Cal 455; Prot 11 g; Carbo 23 g; T Fat 37 g; 72% Calories from Fat; Chol 40 mg; Fiber 4 g; Sod 403 mg; Vit A 48 RE; Vit C 55 mg; Ca 176 mg; Iron 1 mg

French Potato Salad

Recipe furnished by Belle Kuisine of Richmond, Virginia.

2	pounds new potatoes	1	teaspoon finely chopped garlic
•	Salt to taste	•	Freshly cracked pepper to taste
6	tablespoons olive oil	¼	cup dry white wine
1	tablespoon white vinegar		
½	cup chopped red onion		
¼	cup finely chopped fresh parsley		

Combine the potatoes with enough lightly salted water to cover in a saucepan. Bring to a boil. Boil for 20 minutes or until the potatoes are tender but firm; drain. Cool just until the potatoes are easily handled. The salad should be assembled while the potatoes are still warm.

Whisk the olive oil, white vinegar, onion, parsley, garlic, salt and pepper in a bowl and mix well. Peel the potatoes if desired and cut into ½-inch slices. Layer the potatoes in a shallow serving bowl, drizzling each layer with the white wine. Pour the dressing over the potatoes and toss to mix. *Yield: 6 servings.*

Approx Per Serving: Cal 245; Prot 4 g; Carbo 30 g; T Fat 14 g; 45% Calories from Fat; Chol <1 mg; Fiber 3 g; Sod 6 mg; Vit A 26 RE; Vit C 35 mg; Ca 32 mg; Iron 2 mg

Complex carbohydrates such as whole grains, fruits, and vegetables are naturally low in fat and sodium, cholesterol-free, high in fiber, and high in essential vitamins and minerals. Green leafy vegetables, orange vegetables, citrus fruits, melons, and strawberries are rich in vitamin C and beta carotene. Both fiber and certain vitamins may have a protective effect against heart disease. Fiber intake should be aimed at twenty-five grams per day. To increase fiber intake, check the dietary fiber amounts listed on food labels and choose those products that provide higher amounts.

Every mixed green salad starts with some type of greens. Why restrict yourself to head or leaf lettuce salad-after-salad? Be adventuresome. Use other salad plants such as romaine, endive, chicory, escarole, and watercress. And try other uncooked green vegetable leaves too. Spinach, kale, beet and turnip tops, Swiss chard, and dandelion greens make excellent salads. They are rich in vitamins and have a zesty taste. In choosing greens, remember that the darker the salad vegetables are, the richer they are in vitamin A, vitamin C, and iron.

Winter Salad

Raspberry Vinaigrette

¼ cup extra-virgin olive oil
1½ tablespoons fresh lime juice
1½ tablespoons raspberry vinegar

1 tablespoon (scant) honey
½ teaspoon dry mustard
• Salt and pepper to taste

Salad

2 tablespoons chopped walnuts
2½ cups spinach leaves
2½ cups mixed salad greens
• Sections of 1 large grapefruit, seeded

⅓ cup bean sprouts
3 green onions, chopped, or 2 slices red onion
3 or 4 mushrooms, sliced
½ small red bell pepper, julienned

For the vinaigrette, whisk the olive oil, lime juice, raspberry vinegar, honey, dry mustard, salt and pepper in a bowl until blended.

For the salad, spread the walnuts in a single layer on a baking sheet. Toast at 350 degrees for 10 to 20 minutes or until light brown, stirring frequently. Let stand until cool.

Tear the spinach and salad greens into a salad bowl. Add the grapefruit sections, bean sprouts, green onions, mushrooms and bell pepper and mix well. Add the vinaigrette and toss to coat. Sprinkle with the walnuts.
Yield: 4 servings.

Approx Per Serving: Cal 245; Prot 7 g; Carbo 22 g; T Fat 17 g; 56% Calories from Fat; Chol 0 mg; Fiber 7 g; Sod 157 mg; Vit A 1450 RE; Vit C 99 mg; Ca 214 mg; Iron 4 mg

Heart-Healthy French Dressing

1	cup reduced-sodium vegetable juice cocktail	⅛	teaspoon basil
1	tablespoon white vinegar	⅛	teaspoon dry mustard
2	tablespoons flax seed oil	⅛	teaspoon garlic powder
1	teaspoon onion flakes	⅛	teaspoon pepper

Combine the vegetable juice cocktail, white vinegar, flax seed oil, onion flakes, basil, dry mustard, garlic powder and pepper in a jar with a tight-fitting lid. Shake to mix. Store, covered, in the refrigerator. Drizzle over your favorite salad greens. *Yield: 8 (2-tablespoon) servings.*

Approx Per Serving: Cal 44; Prot <1 g; Carbo 3 g; T Fat 3 g; 71% Calories from Fat; Chol <1 mg; Fiber <1 g; Sod 19 mg; Vit A 31 RE; Vit C 8 mg; Ca 6 mg; Iron <1 mg

Quick and Easy Raspberry Vinaigrette

½	cup raspberry vinegar	½	teaspoon minced garlic
½	cup olive oil	•	Salt and pepper to taste
1	tablespoon Dijon mustard		

Whisk the raspberry vinegar, olive oil, Dijon mustard, garlic, salt and pepper in a bowl. Store, covered, in the refrigerator. Drizzle over chilled mixed salad greens. *Yield: 8 (2-tablespoon) servings.*

Approx Per Serving: Cal 128; Prot <1 g; Carbo 1 g; T Fat 14 g; 93% Calories from Fat; Chol 0 mg; Fiber <1 g; Sod 48 mg; Vit A <1 RE; Vit C 1 mg; Ca 4 mg; Iron <1 mg

Salad dressings are a hidden source of fat and sodium, whether on the salad bar or in recipes. Some substitutions can be just as tasteful. Try these reduced-fat alternatives. Substitute 1 cup plain nonfat yogurt for 1 cup mayonnaise; for 1 cup sour cream, substitute 1 cup dry curd cottage cheese blended with lemon juice and skim milk until of the desired consistency or 1 cup plain nonfat yogurt; for regular cream cheese, substitute half the amount or use nonfat cream cheese or whipped part-skim ricotta cheese; substitute 3 tablespoons nonfat Italian salad dressing for 3 tablespoons Italian salad dressing. Be sure to read the label for sugar and sodium content.

Avocado Dressing

Try Avocado Dressing over assorted mixed fresh greens. Mash 1 large ripe avocado. Combine with 2 tablespoons vegetable oil, 1 tablespoon lemon juice, 1/2 teaspoon salt and a dash of pepper, chili powder and garlic powder in a blender. Process until the desired consistency. Yield: 1 cup.

REGENCY DRESSING

1/4	cup vegetable oil	1	egg yolk, lightly beaten
1	tablespoon finely chopped onion	•	Salt and pepper to taste
1	garlic clove	1/4	cup vegetable oil
1/2	cup vinegar	2	cups chicken stock
2	tablespoons Dijon mustard	1	tablespoon flour

Process 1/4 cup oil, onion and garlic in a blender until puréed. Pour into a bowl. Stir in the vinegar, Dijon mustard, egg yolk, salt and pepper. Add 1/4 cup oil gradually, whisking constantly.

Bring 1 1/2 cups of the chicken stock to a boil in a saucepan. Stir in a mixture of the remaining 1/2 cup stock and flour. Cook over medium heat for 5 minutes, stirring constantly. Add the hot stock mixture to the vinegar mixture gradually, whisking constantly until blended. Cool to room temperature. Store, covered, in the refrigerator.
Yield: 24 (2-tablespoon) servings.

Approx Per Serving: Cal 47; Prot <1 g; Carbo 1 g; T Fat 5 g; 91% Calories from Fat; Chol 9 mg; Fiber <1 g; Sod 89 mg; Vit A 4 RE; Vit C <1 mg; Ca 4 mg; Iron <1 mg

ZERO SALAD DRESSING

½ cup tomato juice or reduced-sodium vegetable juice cocktail
2 tablespoons lemon juice
1 tablespoon minced onion
1 tablespoon minced green bell pepper

1 tablespoon parsley flakes
½ teaspoon prepared horseradish
⅛ teaspoon dry mustard
⅛ teaspoon pepper
⅛ teaspoon garlic powder

Combine the tomato juice, lemon juice, onion, bell pepper, parsley flakes, prepared horseradish, dry mustard, pepper and garlic powder in a jar with a tight-fitting lid. Shake to mix. Store, covered, in the refrigerator. Drizzle over mixed salad greens. *Yield: 6 (2-tablespoon) servings.*

Approx Per Serving: Cal 8; Prot <1 g; Carbo 2 g; T Fat <1 g; 5% Calories from Fat; Chol 0 mg; Fiber <1 g; Sod 75 mg; Vit A 16 RE; Vit C 9 mg; Ca 6 mg; Iron <1 mg

SAUCY BRUSSELS SPROUTS

1 pound brussels sprouts, cut into halves
1 cup plain yogurt
2 tablespoons Dijon mustard

2 tablespoons honey
2 to 3 teaspoons dillweed
• Salt and pepper to taste

Steam the brussels sprouts until tender; drain. Cover to keep warm. Combine the yogurt, Dijon mustard, honey, dillweed, salt and pepper in a bowl and mix well. Add the brussels sprouts and mix gently. *Yield: 6 servings.*

Approx Per Serving: Cal 87; Prot 4 g; Carbo 15 g; T Fat 2 g; 19% Calories from Fat; Chol 5 mg; Fiber 3 g; Sod 165 mg; Vit A 82 RE; Vit C 65 mg; Ca 98 mg; Iron 2 mg

Cruciferous vegetables, which include the cabbage family members, are linked with helping protect against cancer. Cauliflower is an example of an "other" vegetable included in this group.

Corn Pudding

Thomas Jefferson's tastes were diverse, but he liked simple preparations and natural flavors. The recipe for one of his favorites, Corn Pudding, follows: Combine 2 eggs, 1/2 cup heavy cream, 1 tablespoon melted butter, 1 1/2 teaspoons sugar, 1/4 teaspoon salt and 1/4 teaspoon pepper. Stir in 3 cups fresh corn kernels (about 12 ears). Spoon the corn mixture into a lightly greased 1 1/2-quart baking dish. Bake at 350 degrees for 30 minutes or until set. Let stand for 5 minutes before serving. You may substitute evaporated skim milk for the heavy cream. Yield: 4 servings.

CORN PUDDING

2	(15-ounce) cans whole kernel corn, drained	1/2	teaspoon salt	
3	eggs	1/8	teaspoon pepper	
2	cups half-and-half	1/8	teaspoon nutmeg	
1/4	cup sugar	1/2	cup plain bread crumbs	
		2	tablespoons butter	

Spread the corn in a buttered 9x13-inch baking dish. Beat the eggs in a mixing bowl at medium speed until blended. Add the half-and-half, sugar, salt, pepper and nutmeg. Beat until smooth. Pour over the corn. Sprinkle with the bread crumbs and dot with the butter.

Place the baking dish in a larger baking pan. Add enough boiling water to the larger baking pan to reach halfway up the sides of the baking dish. Bake at 300 degrees for 1 hour or until a wooden pick inserted in the center comes out clean. *Yield: 8 servings.*

Approx Per Serving: Cal 251; Prot 7 g; Carbo 30 g; T Fat 13 g; 43% Calories from Fat; Chol 110 mg; Fiber 2 g; Sod 508 mg; Vit A 143 RE; Vit C 6 mg; Ca 93 mg; Iron 1 mg

IRISH POTATOES

10 Irish potatoes, peeled	½ cup (1 stick) butter, melted
8 ounces nonfat cream cheese, at room temperature	¼ cup chopped chives
	1 garlic clove, minced
1 cup nonfat sour cream	2 teaspoons salt
	• Paprika to taste

Combine the potatoes with enough water to cover in a saucepan. Bring to a boil. Boil for 30 minutes or until tender but firm; drain. Mash the potatoes in a bowl.

Beat the cream cheese in a mixing bowl at medium-high speed until smooth. Add the potatoes, sour cream, butter, chives, garlic and salt. Beat until mixed. Spoon the potato mixture into a lightly buttered 2-quart baking dish. Sprinkle with paprika.

Chill, covered, for 8 to 10 hours; remove cover. Let stand at room temperature for 15 minutes. Bake at 350 degrees for 30 minutes or until heated through. *Yield: 10 servings.*

Approx Per Serving: Cal 224; Prot 8 g; Carbo 28 g; T Fat 9 g; 37% Calories from Fat; Chol 27 mg; Fiber 2 g; Sod 694 mg; Vit A 224 RE; Vit C 25 mg; Ca 110 mg; Iron 1 mg

Thomas Jefferson, the agrarian gentleman and gourmet taster, who served as governor of Virginia and minister to France before becoming president, probably did more than any other southerner in our history to establish the importance of food in culture.

Root Vegetable and Potato Purée with Pears

Purée or mash potatoes, sweet potatoes, and other vegetables with milk or some of the remaining cooking liquid. Go easy on the butter or margarine. Boost flavor and nutrients by blending in some shredded carrots or zucchini. Cook vegetables by steaming, stir-frying, simmering, or microwaving. If you really enjoy the crispness of French fries and onion rings, try oven baking instead of frying, thus cutting the fat grams.

¼ cup lemon juice
¼ cup water
2 ripe pears or apples, peeled, cut into eighths
1 pound root vegetables (carrots, parsnips or turnips)
1 pound sweet potatoes or white potatoes

¼ cup chicken broth
2 tablespoons (or more) orange juice
1 teaspoon grated lemon zest (optional)
1 teaspoon grated orange zest (optional)
• Salt and white pepper to taste (optional)

Combine the lemon juice and water in a bowl and mix well. Add the pears and stir to coat. Peel the root vegetables and sweet potatoes and cut into large uniform pieces. Arrange in a large baking dish. Drain the pears, reserving ¼ cup of the liquid. Add the pears to the baking dish. Drizzle the reserved liquid over the prepared layers.

Roast, covered, at 425 degrees for 35 minutes or until the vegetables and pears are tender. Let stand until cool.

Process the vegetable mixture in a food processor or blender until mixed. Add the broth and orange juice. Process until puréed or of the desired consistency. Add the lemon zest, orange zest, salt and white pepper. Process just until blended. Serve immediately.

To prepare in advance, transfer the vegetable mixture to a baking dish sprayed with nonstick cooking spray. Chill, covered, until just before serving. Reheat, covered, in a 350-degree conventional oven for 30 to 40 minutes or microwave for 6 minutes. If using white potatoes, use a food mill for puréeing to prevent potatoes from becoming gummy. *Yield: 6 servings.*

Approx Per Serving: Cal 119; Prot 2 g; Carbo 29 g; T Fat <1 g; 3% Calories from Fat; Chol 0 mg; Fiber 5 g; Sod 64 mg; Vit A 3133 RE; Vit C 28 mg; Ca 41 mg; Iron 1 mg

SPINACH SOUFFLE

2 (10-ounce) packages frozen
   chopped spinach, thawed,
   drained
½ to ¾ cup shredded
   reduced-fat
   Cheddar cheese
½ cup reduced-fat
   mayonnaise

½ cup finely minced onion
2 eggs, beaten
¼ teaspoon nutmeg
⅛ teaspoon pepper
⅛ teaspoon salt
⅛ teaspoon garlic powder

Press the spinach to remove the excess moisture. Combine the cheese,
mayonnaise, onion, eggs, nutmeg, pepper, salt and garlic powder in a bowl
and mix well. Stir in the spinach.

Spoon the spinach mixture into a 9x9-inch or 9x13-inch baking dish
sprayed with nonstick cooking spray. Bake at 350 degrees for 30 minutes.
Yield: 6 servings.

Approx Per Serving: Cal 151; Prot 9 g; Carbo 11 g; T Fat 8 g; 48% Calories from Fat;
Chol 83 mg; Fiber 3 g; Sod 331 mg; Vit A 766 RE; Vit C 27 mg; Ca 254 mg; Iron 2 mg

*The FDA advises all
consumers to take
these precautions with
sprouts. Cook sprouts
to significantly reduce
the risk of illness.
Check sandwiches
and salads from
restaurants and delis
for raw sprouts, and
consider requesting
that raw sprouts be
omitted. Be aware that
sprouts grown under
clean conditions in the
home also present a
risk because bacteria
may be present in the
seeds. This advice is
particularly important
for children, the
elderly, and persons
with weakened
immune systems, all of
whom are at high risk
of developing serious
illness due to food-
borne disease. Sprouts
can cause potentially
dangerous salmonella
and E. coli 0157
infection.*

SQUASH GRATIN

2	pounds yellow squash, thinly sliced	8	ounces white Cheddar cheese, shredded
1	medium onion, thinly sliced	½	cup milk
1	teaspoon salt	2	eggs, lightly beaten
•	Freshly ground pepper to taste	2	tablespoons sugar
		1	to 2 tablespoons butter

Blanch the squash and onion in boiling water in a saucepan for 2 to 3 minutes or until tender; drain. Arrange the squash mixture in a 2-quart baking dish. Sprinkle with the salt and pepper.

Combine the cheese, milk, eggs and sugar in a bowl and mix well. Pour over the squash mixture. Dot with the butter. Bake at 350 degrees for 45 minutes. Cut into squares to serve. *Yield: 6 servings.*

Approx Per Serving: Cal 277; Prot 14 g; Carbo 14 g; T Fat 19 g; 60% Calories from Fat; Chol 124 mg; Fiber 3 g; Sod 696 mg; Vit A 209 RE; Vit C 24 mg; Ca 340 mg; Iron 1 mg

VALLEY SWEET POTATOES

A farm recipe from Freestone Valley. This recipe has been made by the postmistress and storekeeper for more than eighty years.

3	cups canned sweet potatoes	1	teaspoon vanilla extract
1	cup sugar	½	teaspoon salt
½	cup skim milk	1	cup packed brown sugar
¼	cup (½ stick) margarine, softened	1	cup chopped pecans
2	eggs, lightly beaten	1	cup shredded coconut
		¼	cup (½ stick) margarine, melted

Mash the sweet potatoes in a bowl. Stir in the sugar, skim milk, ¼ cup margarine, eggs, vanilla and salt. Spoon into a greased 9x13-inch baking pan. Combine the brown sugar, pecans, coconut and ¼ cup margarine in a bowl and mix well. Sprinkle over the top of the prepared layer.

Bake at 350 degrees for 30 minutes or until bubbly. Serve immediately. *Yield: 12 servings.*

Approx Per Serving: Cal 373; Prot 3 g; Carbo 53 g; T Fat 18 g; 42% Calories from Fat; Chol 36 mg; Fiber 3 g; Sod 254 mg; Vit A 425 RE; Vit C 6 mg; Ca 49 mg; Iron 1 mg

Salt is comprised of sodium and chloride, both important minerals required by your body. Sodium is especially necessary for fluid and blood pressure balance. Too much sodium in the diet may cause fluid retention, resulting in edema of the ankles, feet, hands, and eyelids, and shortness of breath. Hypertension can also be affected by dietary sodium. Both fluid retention and hypertension are damaging to your heart and kidneys.

ZUCCHINI MEDLEY

2	cups chopped zucchini		1	cup chopped yellow or white onion
2	cups chopped yellow squash		1	teaspoon oregano
3/4	cup herb-seasoned croutons for stuffing		1	teaspoon pepper
			1	teaspoon salt
4	ounces mozzarella cheese, shredded		2	cups chopped peeled fresh or canned tomatoes
4	ounces sharp Cheddar cheese, shredded		3	tablespoons squeeze margarine

Toss the zucchini, yellow squash, croutons, mozzarella cheese, Cheddar cheese, onion, oregano, pepper and salt in a bowl. Spoon ⅔ of the squash mixture into a greased 9x13-inch baking dish. Layer with the tomatoes. Top with the remaining squash mixture. Drizzle with the margarine.

Place the baking dish on the middle rack of the oven. Bake at 350 degrees for 35 to 40 minutes or until brown and bubbly. Let stand for 5 minutes before serving. *Yield: 6 servings.*

Approx Per Serving: Cal 239; Prot 11 g; Carbo 12 g; T Fat 17 g; 63% Calories from Fat; Chol 35 mg; Fiber 3 g; Sod 708 mg; Vit A 208 RE; Vit C 23 mg; Ca 261 mg; Iron 1 mg

Mabry Mill

Rising Blue Ridge

An Old Receipt for Baked Indian Meal Pudding

Boil one quart of milk, mix in it two gills and a half of corn meal very smoothly, seven eggs well beaten, a gill of molasses, and a good piece of butter; bake it two hours. (1 gill equals 4 ounces)

The Virginia House-wife, 1824
Mary Randolph

In her dissertation on historical Virginia cuisines, Dr. Maryellen Spencer writes that the English settlers of the seventeenth century found the Indian maize easy to plant, process, and use for different foods. The use of corn was adopted by the English and continues to be a popular grain; it is used for corn bread, cracklin' bread, griddle cakes, and corn muffins. Other popular corn foods are hominy, roasting ears, Indian pudding, and the corn pone. Cornbread cakes were cooked over an open fire on the blade of a garden hoe and thus called hoecakes and ashcakes.

Mountain Staff of Life

The use of wheat flour gave us an array of products: Sally Lunn, French rolls, English muffins, loaf breads, and other muffins. There are many stories of Sally Lunn, a tasty bun; it is believed to be among the first receipts, along with syllabub, to be prepared by the Jamestown settlers to remind them of England. Also there is the story that the bread was named after an English girl who sold the bread in Bath, England. The recipe for Sally Lunn continues to be printed in many Virginia cookbooks.

When the early settlers came to Virginia with their English recipes, they found new foods but they did not find recipes for their use. The early leavening agents for some breads were baking soda and buttermilk. For other breads, yeast was obtained from the froth that forms on the top of fermenting ale or beer. The following recipe was an old one for making yeast: Add a pint of hops, 4 potatoes, salt and potatoes. No other instructions were given.

Author Joseph E. Dabney wrote about the Mountain Corn Bread and called it the "Mountain Staff of Life." He states that nothing is more authentically Appalachian than steaming corn bread with fresh vegetables and milk. The Blue Ridge's Thomas Jefferson never lost his love for corn bread, and he grew corn in his garden during his stay in France. Other favorite Appalachian breads were biscuits, Sally Lunn, sweet potato biscuits, angel biscuits, and spoonbread.

Apoquiniminc Cakes or Beaten Biscuits
An early favorite bread was Apoquiniminc Cakes or Beaten Biscuits.

Put a little salt, one egg beaten, and four ounces of butter, in a quart of flour— make it into a paste with new milk, beat it for half an hour with a pestle, roll the paste thin and cut into round cakes; bake them on the gridiron.

The Virginia House-wife, 1824
Mary Randolph

Angel Biscuits

1	envelope dry yeast	1	teaspoon baking soda
2	tablespoons lukewarm water	1	teaspoon salt
5	cups flour	1	cup shortening
¼	cup sugar	¾	cup buttermilk
1	tablespoon baking powder		

Dissolve the yeast in the lukewarm water in a small bowl. Sift the flour, sugar, baking powder, baking soda and salt into a bowl and mix well. Cut in the shortening until crumbly.

Combine the yeast mixture and buttermilk in a bowl and mix well. Add to the flour mixture, stirring until blended. Turn the dough onto a lightly floured surface.

Roll ½ inch thick and cut with a round biscuit cutter. Arrange the biscuits on a nonstick baking sheet. Bake at 400 degrees for 15 minutes or until light brown. *Yield: 2 dozen biscuits.*

Approx Per Biscuit: Cal 183; Prot 3 g; Carbo 23 g; T Fat 9 g; 44% Calories from Fat; Chol <1 mg; Fiber 1 g; Sod 219 mg; Vit A 1 RE; Vit C <1 mg; Ca 47 mg; Iron 1 mg

The 1998 Recommended Dietary Reference Intakes (DRI) for calcium for children under nine are 800 milligrams per day. Youth between nine and eighteen years of age need about 1300 milligrams daily for rapid growth. The recommendation for adults nineteen to fifty years is about 1000 milligrams. For adults over fifty, 1200 milligrams is recommended. Pregnant teens need more than 1200 milligrams of calcium for their own growth as well as for the growth of their baby. Exercise is also recommended to prevent osteoporosis.

CHIVE BISCUITS

4	cups sifted flour	5	tablespoons minced fresh chives
4	teaspoons baking powder	1/8	teaspoon minced fresh rosemary
2	teaspoons salt	1/8	teaspoon garlic powder
6	tablespoons (3/4 stick) butter	1 1/3	cups milk

Sift the flour, baking powder and salt into a bowl and mix well. Cut in the butter until crumbly. Add the chives and rosemary and mix well.

Stir the garlic powder into the milk. Add to the flour mixture, stirring until a soft dough forms. Roll 1/2 inch thick on a lightly floured surface. Cut with a floured round biscuit cutter.

Arrange the biscuits on a nonstick baking sheet. Bake at 450 degrees for 12 to 15 minutes or until light brown. *Yield: 2 dozen biscuits.*

Approx Per Biscuit: Cal 104; Prot 2 g; Carbo 16 g; T Fat 4 g; 31% Calories from Fat; Chol 10 mg; Fiber 1 g; Sod 311 mg; Vit A 34 RE; Vit C <1 mg; Ca 66 mg; Iron 1 mg

Sweet Potato Biscuits

Especially wonderful for a ladies' luncheon or tea.

1 pound sweet potatoes, cooked, peeled	1 cup packed light brown sugar
2½ cups baking mix	¼ cup water

Mash the sweet potatoes in a bowl. Stir in the baking mix, brown sugar and water; the dough will be moist. Turn the dough onto a hard surface dusted with additional biscuit mix. Knead 5 times, adding additional biscuit mix if needed to make an easily handled dough.

Pat the dough ¾ to 1 inch thick. Cut with a 2-inch cutter. Arrange the biscuits on a nonstick baking sheet or baking stone. Bake at 425 degrees for 10 to 12 minutes or until light brown. Serve immediately.
Yield: 3 dozen biscuits.

Approx Per Biscuit: Cal 70; Prot 2 g; Carbo 16 g; T Fat <1 g; 2% Calories from Fat; Chol 0 mg; Fiber 1 g; Sod 92 mg; Vit A 167 RE; Vit C 2 mg; Ca 21 mg; Iron <1 mg

Grandma's Beaten Biscuits

Sift 4 cups flour, 1 teaspoon salt and 1 teaspoon baking powder together. Cut in 1 tablespoon shortening until crumbly. Add 1¾ cups ice water, stirring until blended. Knead until smooth. Turn the dough onto a lightly floured surface and pat with a wooden rolling pin for 20 minutes or until the dough blisters, folding it together as it spreads on the surface. Roll ¼ inch thick; cut with a round biscuit cutter. Arrange the biscuits on a baking sheet and prick the tops with a fork. Bake in a moderately hot oven for 15 minutes or until light brown.

Old-Fashioned Corn Bread

Preheat a lightly greased cast-iron skillet until hot. Mix 1½ cups buttermilk, 1¼ teaspoons baking soda, 1 teaspoon salt and 1 beaten egg until blended. Add 1½ cups (about) cornmeal gradually, stirring constantly until a thin batter forms. Pour into the prepared skillet. Bake at 425 degrees until brown.

CORN BREAD FRUIT STUFFING

1	medium onion, chopped	1	teaspoon sage
1	tart apple, peeled, chopped	1	cup (or more) nonfat chicken broth
¼	cup raisins	4	to 6 cups crumbled corn bread
2	ribs celery, chopped		
1	to 2 teaspoons poultry seasoning		

Sauté the onion, apple, raisins, celery, poultry seasoning and sage in a large skillet coated with nonstick cooking spray for several minutes or until the vegetables are tender, adding a few teaspoons of the broth if needed to keep the mixture from sticking. Add the remaining broth and corn bread and mix well.

Spoon the corn bread mixture into a 2-quart baking dish sprayed with nonstick cooking spray. Bake, covered, at 350 degrees for 30 minutes. You may substitute chopped dried apricots, chopped dried prunes or dried cherries for the raisins and one 8-ounce package corn bread stuffing mix for the corn bread.

For Savory Corn Bread Stuffing, omit the apple and raisins. Stir in ½ cup sliced mushrooms and ¼ cup chopped fresh parsley. Substitute sourdough or French bread cubes for the corn bread.
Yield: 8 (¾-cup) servings.

Approx Per Serving: Cal 274; Prot 7 g; Carbo 45 g; T Fat 8 g; 25% Calories from Fat; Chol 47 mg; Fiber 3 g; Sod 648 mg; Vit A 37 RE; Vit C 2 mg; Ca 69 mg; Iron 2 mg
Nutrition information does not include the Savory Corn Bread Stuffing.

Spoon Bread

1½ cups cornmeal
1⅓ teaspoons salt
1   teaspoon sugar
1½ cups boiling water
¼   cup (½ stick) butter, melted

5   eggs
2   cups milk
1   teaspoon baking powder

Combine the cornmeal, salt and sugar in a bowl and mix well. Stir in the boiling water. Add the butter and mix well.

Whisk the eggs in a bowl until blended. Add the milk and mix well. Stir the egg mixture into the cornmeal mixture. Add the baking powder and mix well. Spoon into a 2-quart baking dish sprayed with nonstick cooking spray. Bake at 350 degrees for 30 to 40 minutes or until brown. *Yield: 10 servings.*

Approx Per Serving: Cal 176; Prot 6 g; Carbo 17 g; T Fat 9 g; 47% Calories from Fat; Chol 125 mg; Fiber 1 g; Sod 467 mg; Vit A 114 RE; Vit C <1 mg; Ca 100 mg; Iron 1 mg

Hoe Cakes

Try this historic recipe for Hoe Cakes. Mix 2 cups cornmeal and ½ teaspoon salt. Stir in ½ cup boiling water. Let stand until the mixture is cool enough to handle. Stir in ½ cup cold water. Shape the cornmeal mixture into oblong cakes. Bake on a greased griddle until brown on both sides, turning once.

CRANBERRY NUT BREAD

Substitute half the all-purpose flour with whole wheat flour, thus adding additional fiber, vitamins, and minerals.

2	cups flour	1	egg, beaten
1	cup sugar	2	cups cranberries,
1½	teaspoons baking powder		cut into halves
½	teaspoon baking soda	½	cup walnut pieces
¼	teaspoon (or less) salt	½	cup shredded
¾	cup orange juice		Cheddar cheese
2	tablespoons shortening, melted		

Combine the flour, sugar, baking powder, baking soda and salt in a bowl and mix well. Combine the orange juice, shortening and egg in a bowl and mix well. Add to the flour mixture, stirring just until moistened. Fold in the cranberries, walnuts and cheese.

Spoon the batter into a greased 5x9-inch loaf pan or 2 miniature loaf pans. Bake at 350 degrees for 1 hour or until the loaf or loaves test done. Cool in pan for 10 minutes. Remove to a wire rack to cool completely.
Yield: 12 servings.

Approx Per Serving: Cal 232; Prot 5 g; Carbo 37 g; T Fat 7 g; 29% Calories from Fat; Chol 23 mg; Fiber 2 g; Sod 198 mg; Vit A 26 RE; Vit C 10 mg; Ca 81 mg; Iron 1 mg

Lemon Nut Bread

1½ cups flour
1 teaspoon baking powder
¼ teaspoon salt
1 cup sugar
½ cup (1 stick) butter, softened
2 eggs, beaten

1 teaspoon lemon extract
½ cup milk
½ cup chopped pecans
• Grated zest and juice of 1 large lemon
⅓ cup sugar

Combine the flour, baking powder and salt in a bowl and mix well. Beat 1 cup sugar and butter in a mixing bowl at medium-high speed until creamy, scraping the bowl occasionally. Add the eggs and flavoring and mix well. Add the dry ingredients alternately with the milk, mixing well after each addition. Fold in the pecans and lemon zest.

Spoon the batter into a greased 5x9-inch loaf pan. Bake at 350 degrees for 1 hour. Drizzle the hot loaf with a mixture of the lemon juice and ⅓ cup sugar. Cool in pan on a wire rack. *Yield: 12 servings.*

Approx Per Serving: Cal 264; Prot 3 g; Carbo 36 g; T Fat 12 g; 41% Calories from Fat; Chol 58 mg; Fiber 1 g; Sod 183 mg; Vit A 91 RE; Vit C 3 mg; Ca 46 mg; Iron 1 mg

To assure that your food is as safe as it is tasty, here are a few tips from our kitchens to yours. Wash your hands, especially after handling raw meat, poultry, or seafood. Don't handle food if your hands have cuts or sores or if you have a cold. Cook meats, eggs, and seafood—the usual suspects when it comes to food poisoning—sufficiently. Surfaces and utensils that come into contact with raw meat, poultry, or seafood should be cleaned before you reuse them. Take raw chops out to the grill on one platter, return them on another. Use separate cutting boards for veggies and raw meats. To keep bacteria at bay, thaw raw meats in the refrigerator, in the kitchen sink inside a sealable plastic bag submerged in very cold water (change the water every thirty minutes), or in the microwave.

*Dietetic Technicians,
Registered (DTRs)
are trained in food and
nutrition and are an
integral part of health
care and food-service
management teams.
DTRs have met the
following criteria to
earn the D.T.R.
credential: Complete
at least a two year
associate's degree
at a US regionally
accredited college or
university. Complete
a dietetic technician
program accredited
by the American
Dietetic Association,
including 450 hours
of supervised practice
experience in various
settings. Pass a
national examination
administered by the
Commission on Dietetic
Registration. Complete
continuing professional
educational require-
ments to maintain
registration.*

SPICY APPLE MUFFINS

A tasty way to add calcium to the diet.

2 cups flour	½ cup 1% milk
½ cup sugar	⅓ cup vegetable oil
1 tablespoon baking powder	½ cup chopped walnuts
1 teaspoon salt	½ cup chopped peeled apple
½ teaspoon baking soda	2 tablespoons brown sugar
½ teaspoon cinnamon	1 tablespoon flour
¼ teaspoon nutmeg	¼ teaspoon cinnamon
1 cup apple or vanilla yogurt	2 tablespoons margarine

Combine 2 cups flour, sugar, baking powder, salt, baking soda, ½ teaspoon cinnamon and nutmeg in a bowl and mix well. Combine the yogurt, 1% milk and oil in a bowl and mix well. Add to the flour mixture, stirring just until moistened. Fold in the walnuts and apple. Fill muffin cups sprayed with nonstick cooking spray ⅔ full.

Combine the brown sugar, 1 tablespoon flour and ¼ teaspoon cinnamon in a bowl and mix well. Cut in the margarine until crumbly. Sprinkle over the top of the muffins. Bake at 400 degrees for 20 to 25 minutes or until light brown. *Yield: 16 muffins.*

Approx Per Muffin: Cal 188; Prot 3 g; Carbo 24 g; T Fat 9 g; 43% Calories from Fat; Chol 2 mg; Fiber 1 g; Sod 308 mg; Vit A 24 RE; Vit C <1 mg; Ca 94 mg; Iron 1 mg

Banana Nut Muffins

1¼ cups all-purpose flour
1 cup whole wheat flour
1½ teaspoons baking soda
1 teaspoon baking powder
¼ teaspoon nutmeg
½ cup skim milk
1½ teaspoons vinegar

1 cup mashed bananas
¾ cup packed brown sugar
⅓ cup canola oil
4 egg whites
1 cup chopped walnuts
   or pecans

Spray 18 muffin cups with nonstick cooking spray. Combine the all-purpose flour, whole wheat flour, baking soda, baking powder and nutmeg in a bowl and mix well. Combine the skim milk and vinegar in a bowl and mix well. Stir in the bananas.

Beat the brown sugar and canola oil in a mixing bowl at medium-high speed until creamy, scraping the bowl occasionally. Add the egg whites. Beat until blended. Add the flour mixture alternately with the banana mixture, mixing well after each addition. Fold in the walnuts.

Fill the prepared muffin cups ⅔ full. Bake at 350 degrees for 20 to 25 minutes or until light brown. *Yield: 18 muffins.*

Approx Per Muffin: Cal 185; Prot 4 g; Carbo 25 g; T Fat 8 g; 40% Calories from Fat; Chol <1 mg; Fiber 2 g; Sod 153 mg; Vit A 6 RE; Vit C 1 mg; Ca 42 mg; Iron 1 mg

How many times have you heard your mother say that breakfast is the healthful way to start the day? Well, she is correct! Listed below are six important benefits of starting your day with breakfast. Breakfast eaters burn more calories throughout the day. Breakfast eaters who consume cereals and fruits in the morning consume less fat and cholesterol each day than breakfast skippers. Starting the day out with breakfast decreases impulsive snacking throughout the day. Breakfast eaters are more likely to get their requirements for calcium and fiber for the day. Eating breakfast helps to improve concentration and work performance throughout the day. Breakfast eaters are less irritable and less fatigued throughout the day than those who skip breakfast.

BLUEBERRY POPPY SEED MUFFINS

2 cups flour	¼ cup (½ stick) margarine, melted
2 tablespoons plus 2 teaspoons sugar	1 egg, beaten
2 teaspoons baking powder	1 teaspoon grated lemon zest
1½ teaspoons poppy seeds	¾ cup fresh blueberries
¼ teaspoon salt	
1 cup milk	

Spray 12 muffin cups with nonstick cooking spray. Combine the flour, sugar, baking powder, poppy seeds and salt in a bowl and mix well. Make a well in the center of the flour mixture. Combine the milk, margarine, egg and lemon zest in a bowl and mix well. Add to the well, stirring just until moistened. Fold in the blueberries.

Fill the prepared muffin cups ⅔ full. Bake at 400 degrees for 15 to 20 minutes or until golden brown. You may substitute thawed, drained frozen blueberries for the fresh blueberries. *Yield: 1 dozen muffins.*

Approx Per Muffin: Cal 147; Prot 4 g; Carbo 21 g; T Fat 5 g; 32% Calories from Fat; Chol 20 mg; Fiber 1 g; Sod 190 mg; Vit A 53 RE; Vit C 2 mg; Ca 82 mg; Iron 1 mg

REFRIGERATOR BRAN MUFFINS

1	cup boiling water	2½	cups flour
1	cup All-Bran cereal	2	cups bran flakes
2	cups buttermilk	1	cup sugar
½	cup (1 stick) margarine, melted	2½	teaspoons baking soda
2	eggs, beaten	1	teaspoon salt

Pour the boiling water over the All-Bran in a heatproof bowl. Whisk the buttermilk, margarine and eggs in a bowl until blended.

Combine the flour, bran flakes, sugar, baking soda and salt in a bowl and mix well. Add to the buttermilk mixture and mix well. Stir in the All-Bran mixture. Fill oiled muffin cups ½ full.

Bake at 400 degrees for 15 minutes or until golden brown. Store the leftover batter, covered, in the refrigerator until just before baking.
Yield: 2 dozen muffins.

Approx Per Muffin: Cal 143; Prot 3 g; Carbo 23 g; T Fat 5 g; 28% Calories from Fat; Chol 18 mg; Fiber 2 g; Sod 311 mg; Vit A 67 RE; Vit C 2 mg; Ca 38 mg; Iron 1 mg

The body absorbs folic acid, the form of the vitamin found in supplements, much more efficiently than folate, the form that is found naturally in foods. Dietary recommendations do take this factor into account. Daily requirements for adults are set at 400 micrograms of "dietary folate equivalents."(The "equivalent" term is used to describe a diet that includes a mixture of folate from foods and fortified foods.) Assume that you will be getting at least some of that supply via breads and cereals, because by law they must now be fortified with folic acid. And aim to secure the rest from foods rich in folate such as spinach, legumes, and oranges, all of which contain many more nutrients and disease-fighting chemicals.

Pumpkin Muffins

Mix muffins with a few light strokes just until the dry ingredients are moistened. Overmixing results in peaks and tunnels in the baked product.

1½ cups flour
½ cup sugar
2 teaspoons baking powder
½ teaspoon cinnamon
½ teaspoon ginger
¼ teaspoon ground cloves
½ cup milk

½ cup canned pumpkin
¼ cup (½ stick) margarine, melted
1 egg, beaten
¼ cup sugar (optional)
½ teaspoon cinnamon (optional)

Sift the flour, ½ cup sugar, baking powder, ½ teaspoon cinnamon, ginger and cloves into a bowl and mix well. Combine the milk, pumpkin, margarine and egg in a bowl and mix well. Add to the flour mixture, stirring just until moistened. Fill muffin cups sprayed with nonstick cooking spray ⅔ full.

Combine ¼ cup sugar and ½ teaspoon cinnamon in a bowl and mix well. Sprinkle over the tops of the muffins. Bake at 400 degrees for 20 to 25 minutes or until golden brown. Serve immediately. *Yield: 1 dozen muffins.*

Approx Per Muffin: Cal 139; Prot 3 g; Carbo 22 g; T Fat 5 g; 30% Calories from Fat; Chol 19 mg; Fiber 1 g; Sod 137 mg; Vit A 198 RE; Vit C 1 mg; Ca 66 mg; Iron 1 mg

OATMEAL BREAD

1	cup quick-cooking oats	2	cups boiling water
½	cup packed brown sugar	1	envelope dry yeast
2	tablespoons margarine	¼	cup lukewarm water
1	tablespoon salt	5	cups flour

Combine the oats, brown sugar, margarine and salt in a bowl and mix well. Stir in the boiling water. Cool to lukewarm. Dissolve the yeast in the lukewarm water in a small bowl.

Stir the yeast mixture into the oats mixture. Add the flour, stirring until an easily handled dough forms. Knead on a lightly floured surface for 5 to 10 minutes or until smooth and elastic. Place the dough in a greased bowl, turning to coat the surface. Let rise, covered, until doubled in bulk.

Punch the dough down. Let rise until doubled in bulk. Divide the dough into 2 equal portions. Shape each portion into a loaf in a greased 5x9-inch loaf pan. Let rise until doubled in bulk.

Bake at 350 degrees for 30 to 40 minutes or until the loaves test done. Remove to a wire rack to cool. Brush the hot loaves with melted margarine if desired for a soft crust. You may substitute honey for the brown sugar. For variety add raisins or your favorite fruit as well as your favorite spices. *Yield: 24 servings.*

Approx Per Serving: Cal 137; Prot 3 g; Carbo 27 g; T Fat 2 g; 10% Calories from Fat; Chol 0 mg; Fiber 1 g; Sod 304 mg; Vit A 10 RE; Vit C 0 mg; Ca 11 mg; Iron 2 mg

Rolled oats and whole wheat are great sources of fiber. Not only do they contain the B-complex vitamins and iron, they also provide other vitamins and minerals lost in processing white all-purpose flour.

SALLY LUNN

Serve with a hearty soup or for afternoon tea.

2	cups milk	2	eggs, beaten
1	yeast cake, or 1 envelope dry yeast	2	tablespoons sugar
		1	teaspoon salt
4	cups flour, sifted	2	tablespoons butter, melted, cooled
¼	cup (½ stick) butter, melted	2	tablespoons sugar

Scald the milk in a saucepan. Cool to lukewarm. Dissolve the yeast in the warm milk and mix well. Combine the yeast mixture, flour, ¼ cup butter, eggs, 2 tablespoons sugar and salt in a bowl and mix until smooth. Pour into a greased 9-inch tube pan. Drizzle with a mixture of 2 tablespoons butter and 2 tablespoons sugar.

Let stand for 1½ to 2 hours or until doubled in bulk. Bake at 350 degrees for 45 minutes or until the loaf pulls from the side of the pan. Remove to a serving platter, topping side up. *Yield: 12 servings.*

Approx Per Serving: Cal 258; Prot 7 g; Carbo 38 g; T Fat 8 g; 29% Calories from Fat; Chol 56 mg; Fiber 1 g; Sod 284 mg; Vit A 82 RE; Vit C <1 mg; Ca 61 mg; Iron 2 mg

WHOLE WHEAT BREAD

³/₄	cup milk	2	envelopes dry yeast
¹/₃	cup shortening	1¹/₂	cups lukewarm water
¹/₃	cup molasses	4¹/₂	cups whole wheat flour
3	tablespoons sugar	2	cups all-purpose flour,
4	teaspoons salt		sifted

Scald the milk in a saucepan. Stir in the shortening, molasses, sugar and salt. Let stand until lukewarm. Dissolve the yeast in the lukewarm water in a bowl and mix well. Stir the milk mixture into the yeast mixture.

Combine the whole wheat flour and all-purpose flour in a bowl and mix well. Add half the flour mixture to the yeast mixture and mix until smooth. Stir in the remaining flour mixture until blended.

Knead the dough on a lightly floured surface until smooth and elastic. Place in a greased bowl, turning to coat the surface. Let rise, covered, in a warm place free of drafts for 1¹/₄ hours or until doubled in bulk. Punch the dough down. Divide the dough into 2 equal portions. Shape each portion into a loaf in a greased 5x9-inch loaf pan.

Let rise, covered, in a warm place free of drafts for 1 hour or until the centers are slightly higher than the edges of the pans. Bake at 400 degrees for 45 to 50 minutes or until the loaves test done. *Yield: 24 servings.*

Approx Per Serving: Cal 164; Prot 5 g; Carbo 30 g; T Fat 4 g; 19% Calories from Fat; Chol 1 mg; Fiber 3 g; Sod 395 mg; Vit A 2 RE; Vit C <1 mg; Ca 28 mg; Iron 2 mg

If you have problems with milk foods, talk with your health care provider. Calcium supplements are available in the form of tablets, powders, and liquids. Since only 10 to 40 percent of the supplement is calcium, one or two pills a day is not sufficient. Also, the calcium in supplements is usually not easily used by the body. Read the label to estimate the amount of calcium in the supplement. Most vitamin-mineral supplements contain very small amounts of calcium.

Easy Refrigerator Yeast Rolls

1¼ cups warm (105- to 115-degree) water
2 envelopes dry yeast
4½ to 5 cups flour

½ cup shortening, melted
½ cup sugar
3 eggs, lightly beaten
2 teaspoons salt

Combine ¼ cup of the warm water and yeast in a 2-cup measuring cup and mix well. Let stand for 5 minutes.

Combine the yeast mixture, remaining 1 cup warm water, 2 cups of the flour, shortening, sugar, eggs and salt in a bowl. Beat with a wooden spoon for 2 minutes. Add enough of the remaining flour to make a soft dough and mix well. Let rise, covered, in a warm place free of drafts for 1 hour.

Punch the dough down. Chill, covered, for 8 to 10 hours. Punch the dough down. Knead 3 or 4 times on a lightly floured surface. Shape the dough into thirty 2-inch balls. Arrange on a lightly greased baking sheet.

Let rise, covered, in a warm place free of drafts for 1½ hours or until doubled in bulk. Bake at 375 degrees for 12 minutes or until golden brown. *Yield: 30 rolls.*

Approx Per Roll: Cal 128; Prot 3 g; Carbo 19 g; T Fat 4 g; 29% Calories from Fat; Chol 21 mg; Fiber 1 g; Sod 162 mg; Vit A 10 RE; Vit C 0 mg; Ca 6 mg; Iron 1 mg

Richmond Capitol Building

RICHMOND CAPITAL EVENTS

An Old Receipt for Sherry Custard

1 quart milk	3 egg yolks
3/4 cup sugar	1 egg
3 tablespoons cornstarch	1 teaspoon rum flavoring
1/8 teaspoon salt	1/2 cup cream sherry

Cook milk, sugar, cornstarch, and salt over medium heat, stirring constantly, until slightly thickened. Beat egg yolks and 1 whole egg. Add 1 cup hot milk mixture to beaten egg yolks, stir and return to hot milk. Continue cooking, stirring constantly, but do not boil, until of custard consistency. Add rum flavoring and sherry. Cool and serve over plain cake.

In the early 1800s the preparation for the Christmas holidays began weeks before the company gathered. The women prepared for the great Christmas dinner: penning up the turkeys to fatten, preparing mince-meat for pies, making all kinds of pickles, saving eggs and butter for cakes, and making spice rounds and the many extra staples that would be needed. Many plantation families traveled into Richmond for the holidays and many would visit for a month. Often weddings were planned around the holidays. Large dinners were served the entire Christmas week.

DESSERTS

Colonial Stack Cakes

The Colonials liked parties, balls, hunts, and weddings.
In the mountains, the Stack Cake was a traditional pioneer wedding cake
put together right at the wedding celebration. Each guest brought a layer of cake.
Applesauce made from either fresh or dried apples (depending on the season)
was spread on each cake layer and the layers were stacked. The bride's popularity
could be measured by the number of stacks she had and the number of layers in each
stack. Since guests were apt to bring different types of cakes, the stacks were
often varicolored and multi-flavored.

Apple Stack Cake

4 cups flour
2 teaspoons baking powder
1 teaspoon salt
$\frac{1}{2}$ teaspoon baking soda
$\frac{3}{4}$ cup shortening
1 cup sugar
1 cup sorghum molasses
3 eggs
1 cup milk
3 cups sweetened spiced applesauce

Sift the flour, baking powder, salt and baking soda together. Beat the shortening
in a mixing bowl until creamy. Add sugar and beat until smooth. Beat in the molasses.
Add the eggs 1 at a time, beating well after each addition. Add the milk and dry
ingredients alternately, mixing well after each addition. Pour the batter $\frac{1}{3}$ inch deep
into 6 or 7 greased 9-inch round cake pans. Bake until golden brown. Let stand until
cool. Stack the layers, spreading the applesauce between each layer.

Yield: 6 or 7 layers

APPLE BROWN BETTY

2 cups chopped peeled
  apples
2 teaspoons butter
2 cups bread crumbs

³/₄ cup packed brown sugar
¹/₄ teaspoon cinnamon
¹/₄ cup hot water

Layer the apples, butter, bread crumbs and brown sugar ½ at a time in a greased 8x8-inch baking pan. Sprinkle with the cinnamon. Pour the hot water over the top; do not stir.

Bake, covered, at 350 degrees for 30 minutes; remove the cover. Bake just until brown. Serve topped with frozen yogurt or whipped topping. *Yield: 6 servings.*

Approx Per Serving: Cal 281; Prot 5 g; Carbo 59 g; T Fat 3 g; 11% Calories from Fat; Chol 3 mg; Fiber 2 g; Sod 334 mg; Vit A 14 RE; Vit C 2 mg; Ca 107 mg; Iron 3 mg

Syllabub

Syllabub was often served at the Governor's Palace in Williamsburg. The old receipt for Syllabub is as follows. Beat 1½ cups chilled strong coffee, 1 cup heavy cream, ½ cup milk and 1 cup aged bourbon with a rotary beater until blended. Stir in ¼ cup (more or less) sugar. Chill. Beat the Syllabub before pouring into small cups or glasses. Yield: 8 servings.

Instead of whipped cream toppings, whip chilled evaporated skim milk with a dash of sugar for a creamy topping. Serve immediately as this topping is less stable. Evaporated skim milk can be used as a substitute in many recipes that call for heavy cream.

APPLE CRISP

10	large apples, peeled, sliced	$\frac{1}{2}$	teaspoon salt
2	cups (or less) sugar	1	egg, beaten
1	cup flour	$\frac{1}{2}$	teaspoon cinnamon
1	teaspoon baking powder	$\frac{1}{4}$	cup ($\frac{1}{2}$ stick) butter

Arrange the apples in a buttered 9x13-inch baking dish. Sprinkle with 1 cup of the sugar.

Combine the remaining 1 cup sugar, flour, baking powder and salt in a bowl and mix well. Add the egg and stir until crumbly. Spoon over the apples. Sprinkle with the cinnamon. Dot with the butter.

Bake at 350 degrees for 50 minutes. Serve topped with whipped cream if desired. *Yield: 12 servings.*

Approx Per Serving: Cal 283; Prot 2 g; Carbo 61 g; T Fat 5 g; 15% Calories from Fat; Chol 28 mg; Fiber 3 g; Sod 182 mg; Vit A 49 RE; Vit C 5 mg; Ca 33 mg; Iron 1 mg

Apple Oat Crunch

1 cup quick-cooking oats	½ cup (1 stick) corn oil
½ cup flour	margarine
⅓ cup packed brown sugar	5 cups sliced peeled apples
½ teaspoon cinnamon	⅓ cup packed brown sugar
¼ teaspoon nutmeg	

Combine the oats, flour, ⅓ cup brown sugar, cinnamon and nutmeg in a bowl and mix well. Cut in the margarine until coarse crumbs form.

Combine the apples and ⅓ cup brown sugar in a bowl and toss to coat. Spoon the apple mixture into a 9x9-inch baking pan sprayed with nonstick cooking spray. Top with the crumb mixture. Bake at 375 degrees for 50 minutes or until brown and bubbly. For variety add raisins and nuts. *Yield: 8 servings.*

Approx Per Serving: Cal 286; Prot 3 g; Carbo 42 g; T Fat 12 g; 38% Calories from Fat; Chol 0 mg; Fiber 3 g; Sod 141 mg; Vit A 117 RE; Vit C 3 mg; Ca 30 mg; Iron 1 mg

Grandmother's Mincemeat

This very old recipe for mincemeat, from about 1875, was handed down through the years from mother to daughter. The ingredients are measured by bowls, and 1 bowl is equal to 1½ cups. Bring 1 bowl vinegar, 1 bowl molasses, 1 bowl grape juice and 2 bowls sugar to a boil. Stir in 5 bowls apples, 1 bowl raisins, 4 bowls ground or chopped cooked pork or beef, 2 tablespoons nutmeg, 1 tablespoon cloves, 1 tablespoon pepper, 1 tablespoon salt and 1 teaspoon cinnamon. Bring to a boil; reduce heat. Cook over low heat until thickened. Use to make pies or cakes.

BANANA PUDDING TRIFLE

1⅓ cups sugar	6 bananas, sliced
¾ cup flour	5 (1.4-ounce) toffee bars, crushed
½ teaspoon salt	
4 cups skim milk	2 cups whipping cream
8 egg yolks	2 tablespoons confectioners' sugar
1 tablespoon vanilla extract	
¼ cup bourbon	1 (1.4-ounce) toffee bar, crushed
2 tablespoons rum	
1 (12-ounce) package vanilla wafers	

Combine the sugar, flour and salt in a large heavy saucepan and mix well. Whisk in the skim milk. Bring to a boil over medium heat, whisking constantly. Remove from heat.

Beat the egg yolks in a mixing bowl at medium-high speed until thick and pale yellow. Stir ¼ of the hot milk mixture into the egg yolks. Stir the egg yolks into the hot milk mixture. Cook for 1 minute, stirring constantly. Stir in the vanilla.

Combine the bourbon and rum in a bowl and mix well. Layer ⅓ of the vanilla wafers in a 4-quart dish. Brush with ⅓ of the bourbon mixture. Layer ⅓ of the bananas, ⅓ of the custard and ⅓ of the 5 toffee bars over the vanilla wafers. Repeat the layering process twice.

Beat the whipping cream in a mixing bowl at high speed until foamy. Add the confectioners' sugar gradually, beating constantly until soft peaks form. Spread over the prepared layers. Sprinkle with 1 toffee bar. Chill, covered, for 3 hours. *Yield: 12 servings.*

Approx Per Serving: Cal 632; Prot 9 g; Carbo 81 g; T Fat 30 g; 41% Calories from Fat; Chol 210 mg; Fiber 2 g; Sod 302 mg; Vit A 300 RE; Vit C 6 mg; Ca 189 mg; Iron 2 mg

DESSERTS

Blueberry Yum-Yum

1	cup sugar	8	ounces nonfat cream cheese, softened
2	tablespoons cornstarch	1	cup sugar
2	quarts fresh blueberries	2	envelopes whipped topping mix
2½	cups graham cracker crumbs	1	cup cold milk
½	cup (1 stick) reduced-fat margarine, softened		

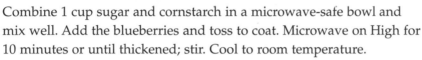

Combine 1 cup sugar and cornstarch in a microwave-safe bowl and mix well. Add the blueberries and toss to coat. Microwave on High for 10 minutes or until thickened; stir. Cool to room temperature.

Combine the graham cracker crumbs and margarine in a bowl and mix well. Combine the cream cheese, 1 cup sugar, topping mix and milk in a mixing bowl. Beat at medium-high speed until blended, scraping the bowl occasionally.

Layer half the crumb mixture and half the cream cheese mixture in the order listed in a shallow dish. Spread with the blueberry mixture. Top with the remaining cream cheese mixture. Sprinkle with the remaining crumb mixture. Chill, covered, for several hours before serving. *Yield: 12 servings.*

Approx Per Serving: Cal 401; Prot 6 g; Carbo 74 g; T Fat 10 g; 21% Calories from Fat; Chol 4 mg; Fiber 3 g; Sod 347 mg; Vit A 132 RE; Vit C 13 mg; Ca 94 mg; Iron 1 mg

Try reducing the amount of sugar in desserts by one-fourth to one-half in order to cut calories. You will be amazed how little the flavor is affected.

Extreme temperatures can lead to surface cracks in cheesecakes. Bake cheesecakes at low temperatures and cool in a draft-free environment.

CHOCOLATE CHEESECAKE

1	(8-ounce) package chocolate wafers, finely crushed	3	tablespoons flour
¼	cup sugar	3	eggs, at room temperature
1	teaspoon cinnamon	2	tablespoons whipping cream
6	tablespoons butter, melted	2	teaspoons vanilla extract
24	ounces cream cheese, softened	¾	cup sour cream
1	cup sugar	¾	teaspoon vanilla extract
1	cup semisweet chocolate chips, melted, cooled	¼	cup semisweet chocolate chips

Combine the chocolate wafer crumbs, ¼ cup sugar and cinnamon in a bowl and mix well. Stir in the butter. Press the crumb mixture over the bottom and up the side of a springform pan. Bake at 400 degrees for 10 minutes. Remove from oven. Let stand until cool. Reduce the oven temperature to 300 degrees.

Beat the cream cheese in a mixing bowl at medium-high speed until creamy. Add 1 cup sugar, 1 cup melted chocolate chips and flour. Beat until smooth and fluffy. Add the eggs 1 at a time, beating well after each addition. Beat in the whipping cream and 2 teaspoons vanilla. Spoon into the prepared pan.

Bake on the middle oven rack at 300 degrees for 60 to 65 minutes or until set. Run a spatula carefully between the side of the pan and the crust; do not remove the side. Spread with a mixture of the sour cream and ¾ teaspoon vanilla. Arrange ¼ cup chocolate chips in a lattice pattern over the top of the cheesecake. Chill, covered, for 2 to 10 hours before serving. May omit the sour cream layer and sprinkle with shaved chocolate.
Yield: 12 servings.

Approx Per Serving: Cal 560; Prot 9 g; Carbo 49 g; T Fat 39 g; 60% Calories from Fat; Chol 141 mg; Fiber 2 g; Sod 363 mg; Vit A 333 RE; Vit C <1 mg; Ca 83 mg; Iron 2 mg

Frozen Mint Cheesecake

24 chocolate wafers, crushed
2   tablespoons sugar
2   tablespoons butter, melted
2   tablespoons water
8   ounces reduced-fat cream cheese, softened
1   (14-ounce) can nonfat sweetened condensed milk
27 hard peppermint candies, crushed
12 ounces frozen light whipped topping, thawed

Combine the wafer crumbs, sugar, butter and water in a bowl and mix well. Press over the bottom of a 9-inch springform pan.

Beat the cream cheese in a mixing bowl at medium-high speed until creamy. Add the condensed milk gradually, beating constantly until smooth. Stir in the candy. Fold in the whipped topping. Spoon into the prepared pan. Freeze, covered, for 6 hours or until firm. Store in the freezer. *Yield: 12 servings.*

Approx Per Serving: Cal 337; Prot 6 g; Carbo 52 g; T Fat 11 g; 29% Calories from Fat; Chol 18 mg; Fiber <1 g; Sod 185 mg; Vit A 60 RE; Vit C <1 mg; Ca 119 mg; Iron 1 mg

CRACKER GOODIES

1	(14-ounce) can sweetened condensed milk	40	butter crackers
1	cup pecans, finely chopped	1	(16-ounce) can ready-to-spread sour cream frosting
1	cup golden raisins		

Combine the condensed milk, pecans and raisins in a saucepan and mix well. Bring to a boil. Boil until thickened, stirring constantly.

Spread 1½ teaspoons of the raisin mixture on each cracker. Arrange the crackers on a nonstick baking sheet. Bake at 250 degrees for 8 to 10 minutes or until bubbly. Let stand until cool. Spread with the frosting. *Yield: 40 servings.*

Approx Per Serving: Cal 125; Prot 1 g; Carbo 18 g; T Fat 6 g; 39% Calories from Fat; Chol 3 mg; Fiber <1 g; Sod 62 mg; Vit A 23 RE; Vit C <1 mg; Ca 35 mg; Iron <1 mg

LEMON CUSTARD

1	cup sugar	1	cup milk
¼	cup (½ stick) butter, softened	•	Juice and zest of 1 large lemon
2	tablespoons flour	2	egg whites
2	egg yolks		

Combine the sugar, butter, flour and egg yolks in a mixing bowl. Beat at medium-high speed until creamy, scraping the bowl occasionally. Add the milk, lemon juice and lemon zest. Beat until mixed.

Beat the egg whites in a mixing bowl until stiff peaks form. Fold into the lemon mixture. Spoon into a 9x9-inch baking pan. Bake at 350 degrees for 30 minutes. *Yield: 6 servings.*

Approx Per Serving: Cal 260; Prot 4 g; Carbo 38 g; T Fat 11 g; 36% Calories from Fat; Chol 97 mg; Fiber <1 g; Sod 119 mg; Vit A 116 RE; Vit C 6 mg; Ca 62 mg; Iron <1 mg

Mrs. Rorer's Cooking School Sauce

Beat ½ cup sugar and ⅓ cup butter or margarine until creamy. Add 2 egg yolks and beat until light and fluffy. Blend in ⅓ cup boiling water, ⅓ cup dry white wine, and a dash of nutmeg. Transfer the mixture to a double boiler. Place over boiling water. (The upper pan should not touch the water.) Cook for 5 minutes or until slightly thickened, stirring constantly. Serve warm or chilled over chopped fresh fruit or drained juice-pack fruit. Yield: 1½ cups.

FRUIT PIZZA

1	(20-ounce) roll sugar cookie dough	2	small peaches, peeled, sliced
1	(4-ounce) package vanilla instant pudding mix	1	kiwifruit, sliced
1	cup milk	1	cup sliced fresh strawberries
8	ounces whipped topping	½	cup fresh blueberries

Press the cookie dough over the bottom and up the side of a 12-inch round pizza pan. Bake at 350 degrees for 15 minutes or until golden brown. Let stand until cool.

Whisk the pudding mix and milk in a bowl until thickened. Fold in the whipped topping. Spread over the baked layer. Arrange the peaches, kiwifruit, strawberries and blueberries in a decorative pattern over the top. Chill, covered, until serving time. Cut into wedges. You may substitute with your favorite fruits. *Yield: 12 servings.*

Approx Per Serving: Cal 290; Prot 3 g; Carbo 43 g; T Fat 11 g; 35% Calories from Fat; Chol 7 mg; Fiber 1 g; Sod 296 mg; Vit A 16 RE; Vit C 14 mg; Ca 33 mg; Iron 1 mg

LAYERED PUDDING DESSERT

1 cup flour
½ cup (1 stick) margarine, melted
8 ounces cream cheese, softened
1 cup confectioners' sugar
1 cup whipped topping

1 (4-ounce) package vanilla instant pudding mix
1 (4-ounce) package chocolate instant pudding mix
2 cups milk
1 cup whipped topping

Combine the flour and margarine in a bowl and mix well. Press over the bottom of a 9x13-inch baking pan. Bake at 350 degrees for 20 minutes or until golden brown. Let stand until cool.

Combine the cream cheese, confectioners' sugar and 1 cup whipped topping in a mixing bowl. Beat at medium speed until smooth, scraping the bowl occasionally. Spread over the baked layer.

Whisk the pudding mixes and milk in a bowl until thickened. Spread over the prepared layers. Top with 1 cup whipped topping. Chill, covered, until set. *Yield: 15 servings.*

Approx Per Serving: Cal 263; Prot 3 g; Carbo 30 g; T Fat 14 g; 49% Calories from Fat; Chol 21 mg; Fiber <1 g; Sod 321 mg; Vit A 128 RE; Vit C <1 mg; Ca 56 mg; Iron 1 mg

Cut calories and fat grams by coating baking pans lightly with nonstick cooking spray rather than butter, margarine, or vegetable oil.

CARAMEL APPLE CAKE

Cake

3	cups flour	1/2	cup packed brown sugar
2	teaspoons cinnamon	3	eggs
1	teaspoon baking soda	3 1/2	cups chopped peeled apples
1/2	teaspoon salt	1	cup chopped walnuts
1/2	teaspoon nutmeg	2	teaspoons vanilla extract
1 1/2	cups vegetable oil		
1 1/2	cups sugar		

Caramel Icing

1/2	cup packed brown sugar	1/8	teaspoon salt
1/3	cup light cream	1	to 1 1/4 cups confectioners' sugar
1/4	cup (1/2 stick) butter or margarine		

For the cake, combine the flour, cinnamon, baking soda, salt and nutmeg in a bowl and mix well. Combine the oil, sugar and brown sugar in a mixing bowl. Beat until blended. Add the eggs 1 at a time, beating well after each addition. Stir in the flour mixture. Fold in the apples, walnuts and vanilla.

Spoon the batter into a greased and floured 10-inch tube pan. Bake at 325 degrees for 1 1/2 hours or until the cake tests done. Cool in pan for 10 minutes. Remove to a wire rack to cool completely.

For the icing, combine the brown sugar, cream, butter and salt in a double boiler over simmering water. Cook until blended, stirring frequently. Cool to room temperature. Add the confectioners' sugar and beat until smooth. Drizzle over the cake. Sprinkle with additional chopped walnuts if desired. *Yield: 16 servings.*

Approx Per Serving: Cal 540; Prot 5 g; Carbo 65 g; T Fat 30 g; 49% Calories from Fat; Chol 51 mg; Fiber 2 g; Sod 219 mg; Vit A 56 RE; Vit C 1 mg; Ca 34 mg; Iron 2 mg

DESSERTS

APRICOT PECAN POUND CAKE

Cake

3	cups flour	6	egg yolks
1/2	teaspoon baking soda	1	cup sour cream
1/2	teaspoon salt	2	teaspoons sherry or maple flavoring
1	cup chopped pecans	1	teaspoon lemon extract
1 1/2	teaspoons flour	1	teaspoon vanilla extract
3	cups sugar	6	egg whites, stiffly beaten
1	cup (2 sticks) butter, softened		
1	(6-ounce) jar baby food apricots		

Butterscotch Icing

2	cups confectioners' sugar	1/2	cup butterscotch chips, melted
1/2	cup (1 stick) butter, softened	1	to 2 tablespoons apricot nectar

For the cake, sift 3 cups flour, baking soda and salt into a bowl 3 times. Toss the pecans with 1 1/2 teaspoons flour in a bowl. Combine the sugar and butter in a mixing bowl. Beat at medium speed until creamy, scraping the bowl occasionally. Add the apricots and beat until blended.

Add the egg yolks 1 at a time, beating well after each addition. Add the flour mixture alternately with the sour cream, beginning and ending with the flour mixture. Stir in the pecans and flavorings. Fold in the egg whites. Spoon the batter into a greased and floured 10-inch tube pan. Bake at 300 degrees for 1 1/2 hours. Cool in pan for 10 minutes. Remove to a wire rack to cool completely.

For the icing, combine the confectioners' sugar, butter, butterscotch chips and apricot nectar in a mixing bowl. Beat until of a drizzling consistency, scraping the bowl occasionally. Drizzle over the cake.
Yield: 16 servings.

Approx Per Serving: Cal 589; Prot 6 g; Carbo 79 g; T Fat 29 g; 44% Calories from Fat; Chol 133 mg; Fiber 1 g; Sod 326 mg; Vit A 236 RE; Vit C 3 mg; Ca 39 mg; Iron 2 mg

Plain Pound Cake

The recipe stated that this cake could be kept for weeks in an earthen jar, closely covered, first dipping letter paper in brandy and placing over the top of the cake before covering the jar. The recipe was given as follows. Beat to a cream one pound of butter with one pound of sugar, after mixing well with the beaten yolks of twelve eggs, one grated nutmeg, one glass of wine, one glass of rose water. Then stir in one pound of sifted flour and the well beaten whites of the eggs. Bake to a nice light brown.

CHOCOLATE ANGEL FOOD CAKE

1½ cups sifted confectioners' sugar
¾ cup cake flour
¼ cup baking cocoa
13 egg whites
1½ teaspoons cream of tartar
¼ teaspoon salt
1 cup sugar

1½ teaspoons vanilla extract
2 cups heavy whipping cream
2 to 4 tablespoons confectioners' sugar
1 (1.5-ounce) chocolate candy bar, shaved

Sift 1½ cups confectioners' sugar, cake flour and baking cocoa into a bowl 3 times. Combine the egg whites, cream of tartar and salt in a mixing bowl. Beat until foamy. Add the sugar 2 tablespoons at a time, beating constantly until stiff peaks form. Fold in the vanilla. Sift the baking cocoa mixture over the meringue and fold in until it disappears.

Spoon the batter gently into a 10-inch angel food cake pan. Cut through the batter with a knife. Bake at 375 degrees for 35 to 45 minutes or until the top springs back when lightly touched. Invert onto a funnel to cool completely. Loosen the cake from the side of the pan. Invert onto a cake plate.

Beat the whipping cream in a mixing bowl until soft peaks form. Add 2 to 4 tablespoons confectioners' sugar and mix well. Cut into 12 slices. Top each serving with the sweetened whipped cream and chocolate shavings. *Yield: 12 servings.*

Approx Per Serving: Cal 333; Prot 6 g; Carbo 43 g; T Fat 16 g; 42% Calories from Fat; Chol 55 mg; Fiber 1 g; Sod 126 mg; Vit A 169 RE; Vit C <1 mg; Ca 36 mg; Iron 1 mg

FUDGE BAR CAKE

Cake

½ cup boiling water
1 ounce unsweetened
   chocolate, chopped
1 cup sifted cake flour
1 cup sugar
1 teaspoon salt
½ teaspoon baking soda

¼ cup milk
1½ teaspoons vinegar
¼ cup shortening or
   margarine
1 egg
½ teaspoon vanilla extract

Fudge Nut Frosting

2 ounces unsweetened
   chocolate, chopped
2 cups sugar
½ cup (1 stick) margarine or
   shortening

⅔ cup milk
½ teaspoon salt
½ cup chopped pecans
1 tablespoon vanilla extract

For the cake, pour the boiling water gradually over the chocolate in a heatproof bowl, stirring constantly until melted. Sift the cake flour, sugar, salt and baking soda into a bowl and mix well. Stir into the chocolate mixture. Let stand until cool.

Combine the milk and vinegar in a small bowl. Add the shortening to the chocolate mixture. Beat with a wooden spoon for 200 strokes. Stir in the milk mixture, egg and vanilla. Beat with a wooden spoon for 100 strokes.

Spoon the batter into a greased and floured 8x8-inch cake pan. Bake at 350 degrees for 35 to 45 minutes or until the cake tests done. Cool in pan on a wire rack.

For the frosting, combine the chocolate, sugar, margarine, milk and salt in a saucepan. Bring to a boil. Boil for 2 to 4 minutes or until thickened, stirring constantly. Remove from heat. Place the saucepan in a sink filled with enough cold water to reach halfway up the side of the saucepan. Stir in the pecans and vanilla. Beat until of a spreading consistency. Spread over the top of the cake immediately. *Yield: 9 servings.*

Approx Per Serving: Cal 558; Prot 4 g; Carbo 80 g; T Fat 27 g; 42% Calories from Fat; Chol 27 mg; Fiber 2 g; Sod 597 mg; Vit A 120 RE; Vit C <1 mg; Ca 48 mg; Iron 2 mg

Toasting nuts intensifies the flavor and thus decreases the amount needed, which in turn decreases the amount of fat grams. For even more flavor, yet less fat, mix in chopped dried fruits.

ONE, TWO, THREE, FOUR CAKE

3	cups flour	2	cups sugar
2	teaspoons baking powder	1	cup (2 sticks) butter, softened
⅛	teaspoon salt		
1	cup milk	4	egg yolks, beaten
1½	teaspoons vanilla extract	4	egg whites

Sift the flour, baking powder and salt together. Mix the milk and vanilla in a small bowl.

Combine the sugar and butter in a mixing bowl. Beat at medium-high speed until creamy, scraping the bowl occasionally. Add the egg yolks and beat until blended. Add the milk mixture alternately with the dry ingredients, mixing well after each addition.

Beat the egg whites in a mixing bowl at high speed until stiff peaks form. Fold the egg whites into the batter. Spoon the batter into a 10-inch tube pan. Bake at 325 degrees for 1 hour. Cool in pan for 10 minutes. Remove to a wire rack to cool completely. *Yield: 16 servings.*

Approx Per Serving: Cal 312; Prot 5 g; Carbo 44 g; T Fat 14 g; 39% Calories from Fat; Chol 86 mg; Fiber 1 g; Sod 220 mg; Vit A 136 RE; Vit C <1 mg; Ca 65 mg; Iron 1 mg

DESSERTS

Sally White Cake

1½	tablespoons (or less) vegetable oil	9	egg yolks, beaten
4	cups flour, sifted	1	teaspoon vanilla extract
1	tablespoon nutmeg	3	(8-ounce) packages frozen grated coconut
2	teaspoons baking powder	2½	cups chopped almonds
½	teaspoon salt	2	cups citron, finely chopped
¼	cup sherry	2	cups candied red cherries, cut into halves
¼	cup brandy	1	cup flour
4	cups (8 sticks) butter or margarine, softened	9	egg whites, stiffly beaten
3	cups sugar		

Coat the side and bottom of a tube pan lightly with some of the oil. Line with parchment paper. Brush with the remaining oil. Sift 4 cups flour, nutmeg, baking powder and salt into a bowl and mix well. Mix the wine and brandy in a bowl.

Beat the butter in a mixing bowl at medium-high speed until creamy, scraping the bowl occasionally. Add the sugar gradually, beating constantly until light and fluffy. Add the egg yolks and beat until blended. Add the flour mixture and wine mixture alternately to the creamed mixture, mixing well after each addition. Beat in the vanilla.

Toss the coconut, almonds, citron and cherries with 1 cup flour in a large bowl. Add the batter and mix well. Fold in the egg whites. Spoon into the prepared pan. Place a baking pan filled with water on the lower shelf of the oven. Place the cake on the middle shelf of the oven.

Bake at 250 degrees for 3 hours or until the cake tests done. Cool in pan for 10 minutes. Remove to a wire rack to cool completely. Store in a tightly covered tin. *Yield: 20 servings.*

Approx Per Serving: Cal 982; Prot 11 g; Carbo 103 g; T Fat 61 g; 56% Calories from Fat; Chol 195 mg; Fiber 6 g; Sod 586 mg; Vit A 386 RE; Vit C 2 mg; Ca 122 mg; Iron 3 mg

Although many families in the colonies had their own herb gardens, herbs and spices were also imported. These were used for cuisine specialties, as preservatives for the food supply, and for special medications. During the 1800s, spices contained large amounts of fibrous or woody materials. Better processing techniques have done much to solve this problem. In the early 1900s many salesmen went from door-to-door selling spices; Golden Rule, Watkins, Raleigh, and McNess were some of the well-known brands.

Experiment a little and lower the fat in some of your favorite old recipes. In baked products, such as brownies, cookies, cakes, muffins, and breads, try substituting an equal amount of applesauce, mashed bananas, or other puréed fruit, or cottage cheese for at least half the oil, butter, or margarine in the recipe. Try substituting buttermilk, nonfat yogurt, or reduced-fat yogurt for sour cream, butter, and margarine when making biscuits, muffins, and other breads.

FAVORITE BAR COOKIES

2	cups packed brown sugar	1	egg, lightly beaten
2	cups flour	1	teaspoon vanilla extract
½	cup (1 stick) margarine, softened	1	cup miniature semisweet chocolate chips
1	teaspoon baking powder	½	cup chopped English walnuts
¼	teaspoon salt		
1	cup milk		

Combine the brown sugar and flour in a bowl and mix well. Cut in the margarine until crumbly. Reserve 1 cup of the crumb mixture.

Stir the baking powder and salt into the remaining crumb mixture. Add the milk, egg and vanilla, stirring with a fork until smooth. Spoon into a lightly oiled 9x13-inch baking pan. Sprinkle with the reserved crumb mixture.

Toss the chocolate chips and walnuts in a bowl. Sprinkle evenly over the prepared layers. Bake at 350 degrees for 35 minutes. Cool in pan on a wire rack. Cut into bars. *Yield: 2 dozen bars.*

Approx Per Bar: Cal 219; Prot 3 g; Carbo 34 g; T Fat 9 g; 35% Calories from Fat; Chol 10 mg; Fiber 1 g; Sod 104 mg; Vit A 45 RE; Vit C <1 mg; Ca 45 mg; Iron 2 mg

DESSERTS

DATE REFRIGERATOR COOKIES

2¼	cups pitted dates, chopped	½	teaspoon salt
1	cup sugar	½	teaspoon baking soda
1	cup water	1	cup shortening
1	cup chopped pecans	2	cups packed brown sugar
4	cups sifted flour	3	eggs, beaten

Combine the dates, sugar and water in a saucepan. Cook over low heat for 10 minutes or until thickened, stirring frequently. Stir in the pecans. Let stand until cool.

Sift the flour, salt and baking soda together. Beat the shortening in a mixing bowl at medium-high speed until creamy. Add the brown sugar. Beat until light and fluffy, scraping the bowl occasionally. Add the eggs and beat until blended. Add the flour mixture and mix well. Chill, covered, until firm.

Roll the dough ¼ inch thick on a lightly floured surface. Spread with the date mixture. Roll as for a jelly roll. Chill, wrapped in waxed paper, for 8 to 10 hours; slice.

Arrange the slices on a nonstick cookie sheet. Bake at 400 degrees until brown. Cool on cookie sheet for 2 minutes. Remove to a wire rack to cool completely. *Yield: 5 dozen cookies.*

Approx Per Cookie: Cal 134; Prot 1 g; Carbo 22 g; T Fat 5 g; 33% Calories from Fat; Chol 11 mg; Fiber 1 g; Sod 36 mg; Vit A 5 RE; Vit C <1 mg; Ca 12 mg; Iron 1 mg

Guard against food-borne illnesses by not consuming raw cookie dough or tasting any meat, poultry, fish, or egg dish while it is raw or partially cooked. Never drink unpasteurized milk or milk products.

Low-Fat Ginger Cookies

Mix 1 package ginger-bread mix, ¼ cup egg substitute, ¼ cup unsweetened applesauce and ¼ cup skim milk by hand until blended. Drop by rounded teaspoonfuls onto a cookie sheet sprayed with nonstick cooking spray. Bake at 350 degrees until light brown. Each cookie contains 1 gram of fat. Yield: 3 dozen cookies.

GINGERBREAD COOKIES

2	cups flour	1	cup sugar
2	teaspoons ginger	¾	cup (1½ sticks) butter,
1	teaspoon baking soda		softened
1	teaspoon cinnamon	¼	cup light molasses
1	teaspoon ground cloves	1	egg
¼	teaspoon salt	⅓	cup sugar

Combine the flour, ginger, baking soda, cinnamon, cloves and salt in a bowl and mix well. Beat 1 cup sugar and butter in a mixing bowl at medium speed until blended. Add the molasses and egg and beat until light and fluffy. Add the flour mixture and mix well. Chill, covered, for 2 hours or until firm.

Shape the dough into 1-inch balls. Roll the balls in ⅓ cup sugar. Arrange 2 inches apart on a greased cookie sheet. Place 1 drop of water on top of each cookie with fingertip; do not press.

Bake at 350 degrees for 12 to 15 minutes or until flat and crinkled. Cool on cookie sheet for 2 minutes. Remove to a wire rack to cool completely. Store in an airtight container. The dough may be stored, covered, in the refrigerator and baked as needed. *Yield: 4 dozen cookies.*

Approx Per Cookie: Cal 72; Prot 1 g; Carbo 11 g; T Fat 3 g; 38% Calories from Fat; Chol 12 mg; Fiber <1 g; Sod 69 mg; Vit A 29 RE; Vit C 0 mg; Ca 5 mg; Iron <1 mg

Molasses Cookies

6	cups flour	1	cup blackstrap molasses
1	tablespoon ginger	1	cup shortening, melted
1	tablespoon baking soda	2	eggs, lightly beaten
1	teaspoon salt	2	tablespoons vinegar
1	cup sugar	½	cup boiling coffee

Combine the flour, ginger, baking soda and salt in a bowl and mix well. Combine the sugar, molasses, shortening, eggs and vinegar in a bowl and mix well. Add the flour mixture alternately with the coffee, mixing well after each addition.

Let stand for 1 hour or chill, covered, in the refrigerator. Roll the dough on a lightly floured surface. Cut with your favorite cookie cutter. Arrange the cookies on a nonstick cookie sheet. Bake at 350 degrees for 9 minutes. Cool on cookie sheet for 2 minutes. Remove to a wire rack to cool completely. *Yield: 6 dozen cookies.*

Approx Per Cookie: Cal 87; Prot 1 g; Carbo 14 g; T Fat 3 g; 32% Calories from Fat; Chol 6 mg; Fiber <1 g; Sod 89 mg; Vit A 3 RE; Vit C <1 mg; Ca 42 mg; Iron 1 mg

Prepare cookie dough in advance and freeze for future use. Use as needed, allowing the dough to thaw in the refrigerator. If you plan to make four or five recipes for gifts or a party, try using one day for mixing the recipes. The next day have a baking day. Pack the cookies in decorative tins or boxes for distribution.

Use two egg whites in place of one whole egg in cookies, breads, pancakes, casseroles, French toast, cheesecakes, puddings, and other recipes that call for whole eggs to decrease cholesterol. Recipes that require egg yolks, such as puff pastry, are best made with whole eggs.

DELUXE OATMEAL COOKIES

Bake your own oatmeal cookies. You can cut the shortening (margarine, butter, or oil) and sugar by at least one-third in many cookie recipes without affecting the quality.

1½ cups flour	1 teaspoon vanilla extract
1 teaspoon baking soda	1½ cups quick-cooking oats
1 cup (2 sticks) butter, softened	1 cup semisweet chocolate chips
¾ cup sugar	1 cup dried cherries or cranberries
¾ cup packed light brown sugar	1 cup toffee bits
1 egg	

Sift the flour and baking soda together. Beat the butter in a mixing bowl at medium-high speed until creamy. Add the sugar and brown sugar. Beat until light and fluffy; do not overbeat. Add the egg and vanilla and beat until blended. Stir in the flour mixture. Fold in the oats, chocolate chips, cherries and toffee bits.

Shape the dough into 3 logs 2 inches in diameter. Chill, wrapped in plastic wrap, for 1 hour or longer. Cut each roll into ½- to ¾-inch slices. Arrange on a nonstick cookie sheet. Bake at 350 degrees for 10 to 12 minutes or until light brown. Cool on cookie sheet for 1 minute. Remove to a wire rack to cool completely. *Yield: 3 dozen cookies.*

Approx Per Cookie: Cal 183; Prot 2 g; Carbo 25 g; T Fat 9 g; 43% Calories from Fat; Chol 25 mg; Fiber 1 g; Sod 121 mg; Vit A 85 RE; Vit C <1 mg; Ca 13 mg; Iron 1 mg

COCONUT CHESS PIE

³/₄	cup shredded coconut	2	eggs, lightly beaten
1	unbaked (9-inch) pie shell	1	tablespoon butter
1	cup milk	1	teaspoon vanilla extract
1	cup sugar		

Spread the coconut over the bottom of the pie shell. Whisk the milk, sugar, eggs, butter and vanilla in a bowl. Pour into the prepared pie shell. Bake at 400 degrees for 30 minutes. *Yield: 8 servings.*

Approx Per Serving: Cal 304; Prot 4 g; Carbo 41 g; T Fat 14 g; 42% Calories from Fat; Chol 61 mg; Fiber 1 g; Sod 185 mg; Vit A 47 RE; Vit C <1 mg; Ca 47 mg; Iron 1 mg

LEMON CHESS PIE

2	cups sugar	¹/₂	cup milk
3	tablespoons flour	•	Juice and grated zest of 2 lemons
¹/₈	teaspoon salt		
3	eggs, beaten	1	unbaked (9-inch) pie shell
2	tablespoons butter, melted		

Combine the sugar, flour and salt in a bowl and mix well. Stir in the eggs and butter. Add the milk, lemon juice and zest and mix well. Pour into the pie shell. Bake at 325 degrees for 45 to 60 minutes or until set.
Yield: 8 servings.

Approx Per Serving: Cal 384; Prot 5 g; Carbo 65 g; T Fat 13 g; 29% Calories from Fat; Chol 90 mg; Fiber 1 g; Sod 214 mg; Vit A 68 RE; Vit C 7 mg; Ca 34 mg; Iron 1 mg

As to the origin of chess pie, it has been speculated that a cook had called it "jes pie" when she was asked what she was cooking. Dabney also wrote that it had been described as pies "baked with so much sugar they could be stored in a pie chest".

Lemon Fluff Pie

1	(3-ounce) package lemon gelatin
1	cup boiling water
½	cup cold water
1	cup nonfat lemon yogurt
8	ounces whipped topping
1	(9-inch) graham cracker pie shell

Dissolve the gelatin in the boiling water in a heatproof bowl. Stir in the cold water. Chill until of the consistency of unbeaten egg whites. Fold in the yogurt and whipped topping. Spoon into the pie shell. Chill, covered, until set. *Yield: 8 servings.*

Approx Per Serving: Cal 303; Prot 4 g; Carbo 41 g; T Fat 13 g; 39% Calories from Fat; Chol <1 mg; Fiber <1 g; Sod 228 mg; Vit A 61 RE; Vit C <1 mg; Ca 61 mg; Iron 1 mg

Lemon Fruit Pies

1	(14-ounce) can nonfat sweetened condensed milk
½	cup lemon juice
12	ounces light whipped topping
1	(11-ounce) can mandarin oranges, drained
1	(8-ounce) can juice-pack pineapple chunks, drained
1	(6-ounce) bottle whole maraschino cherries, drained
½	cup chopped pecans
2	(9-inch) graham cracker pie shells

Combine the condensed milk and lemon juice in a bowl and stir until thickened. Fold in the whipped topping. Add the mandarin oranges, pineapple, maraschino cherries and pecans and mix gently. Spoon into the pie shells. Chill, covered, for 8 to 10 hours. *Yield: 16 servings.*

Approx Per Serving: Cal 329; Prot 4 g; Carbo 50 g; T Fat 13 g; 35% Calories from Fat; Chol 2 mg; Fiber 1 g; Sod 198 mg; Vit A 78 RE; Vit C 9 mg; Ca 83 mg; Iron 1 mg

Key Lime Pie

1 (14-ounce) can
  nonfat sweetened
  condensed milk
12 ounces whipped topping

¼ to ½ cup Key lime juice
1 (9-inch) graham cracker
  pie shell, baked

Combine the condensed milk, whipped topping and lime juice in a bowl and mix well. Spoon into the pie shell. Chill, covered, for 8 to 10 hours.
Yield: 8 servings.

Approx Per Serving: Cal 423; Prot 6 g; Carbo 61 g; T Fat 16 g; 34% Calories from Fat; Chol 3 mg; Fiber 1 g; Sod 223 mg; Vit A 61 RE; Vit C 5 mg; Ca 147 mg; Iron 1 mg

Southern Peanut Pie

3 eggs
1½ cups dark corn syrup
½ cup sugar
¼ cup (½ stick) butter,
  melted
½ teaspoon vanilla extract

¼ teaspoon salt
1½ cups chopped roasted
  peanuts
1 unbaked (10-inch)
  deep-dish pie shell

Beat the eggs in a mixing bowl at medium speed until foamy. Add the corn syrup, sugar, butter, vanilla and salt. Beat until blended. Stir in the peanuts. Pour into the pie shell.

Bake at 375 degrees for 50 to 55 minutes or until set. Serve warm or at room temperature topped with whipped cream or ice cream.
Yield: 6 servings.

Approx Per Serving: Cal 767; Prot 15 g; Carbo 99 g; T Fat 37 g; 42% Calories from Fat; Chol 127 mg; Fiber 2 g; Sod 496 mg; Vit A 119 RE; Vit C 0 mg; Ca 59 mg; Iron 2 mg

Fats, oils, and sweets represent the smallest portion of the Food Guide Pyramid. Moderation of rich treats is the key. All foods fit into the food pyramid.

Guiltless Pineapple Pies

Instead of using flaky pastry shells with their high fat content, make desserts with graham cracker crumb crusts. Prepare the crusts with half the butter or margarine called for in the recipe. If additional butter or margarine is needed, add just enough to moisten the crumbs.

1 (20-ounce) can juice-pack crushed pineapple, drained

1 (15-ounce) can juice-pack crushed pineapple, drained

1 (14-ounce) can nonfat sweetened condensed milk

8 ounces light whipped topping

¼ cup lemon juice

2 (9-inch) reduced-fat graham cracker pie shells

Combine the crushed pineapple, condensed milk, whipped topping and lemon juice in a bowl and mix gently. Spoon into the pie shells. Chill, covered, for 1 hour. *Yield: 16 servings.*

Approx Per Serving: Cal 225; Prot 3 g; Carbo 40 g; T Fat 5 g; 20% Calories from Fat; Chol 2 mg; Fiber 1 g; Sod 122 mg; Vit A 1 RE; Vit C 7 mg; Ca 79 mg; Iron 1 mg

Pumpkin Pie

Perhaps more than anything else at a holiday meal, dessert has a traditional feel. Try this lighter version of the traditional pumpkin pie.

Gingersnap Crust

2 tablespoons margarine, melted	1 cup gingersnap crumbs

Pumpkin Pie

2 envelopes unflavored gelatin	¾ cup plain nonfat yogurt
1 cup evaporated skim milk	2 eggs whites, at room temperature
1 cup canned pumpkin	⅛ teaspoon salt
½ teaspoon pumpkin pie spice	⅔ cup packed brown sugar
¼ teaspoon grated orange zest	1 tablespoon chopped pecans, toasted

For the crust, combine the margarine and gingersnap crumbs in a small bowl. Press the crumb mixture into a 9-inch pie plate sprayed with nonstick cooking spray.

For the pie, sprinkle the gelatin over the evaporated skim milk in a heavy saucepan. Let stand for 1 minute. Cook over low heat until the gelatin dissolves, stirring constantly. Stir in the pumpkin, pumpkin pie spice and zest. Chill until of the consistency of egg whites. Fold in the yogurt.

Beat the egg whites and salt in a mixing bowl at medium speed until soft peaks form. Add the brown sugar gradually, beating constantly until stiff peaks form. Fold the egg white mixture into the pumpkin mixture. Spoon into the prepared pie plate. Chill, covered, until set. Sprinkle with the pecans just before serving. *Yield: 8 servings.*

Approx Per Serving: Cal 211; Prot 7 g; Carbo 36 g; T Fat 5 g; 20% Calories from Fat; Chol 2 mg; Fiber 2 g; Sod 231 mg; Vit A 514 RE; Vit C 2 mg; Ca 160 mg; Iron 1 mg

As another pastry option, prepare single-crust pies. Either make open-faced or arrange the fruit in the pie plate and top with pastry.

Pumpkin Nut Pies

1½ cups packed brown sugar or granulated sugar	2 cups milk
2 tablespoons flour	2 egg yolks, lightly beaten
1 teaspoon cinnamon	¼ cup shredded coconut
½ teaspoon salt	¼ cup chopped pecans
½ teaspoon nutmeg	2 egg whites
½ teaspoon ginger	2 unbaked (10-inch) deep-dish pie shells, chilled
1 (15-ounce) can pumpkin	

Combine the brown sugar, flour, cinnamon, salt, nutmeg and ginger in a bowl and mix well. Stir in the pumpkin. Add the milk and egg yolks and mix well. Stir in the coconut and pecans.

Beat the egg whites in a mixing bowl until stiff peaks form. Fold into the pumpkin mixture. Spoon the pumpkin mixture into the pie shells. Bake at 450 degrees for 10 minutes. Reduce the heat to 350 degrees. Bake for 30 to 45 minutes longer or until set. Let stand until cool. Serve topped lightly with whipped cream. You may bake in three 9-inch pie shells. Rounded measurements of the cinnamon, nutmeg and ginger produce a spicier pie. *Yield: 16 servings.*

Approx Per Serving: Cal 268; Prot 5 g; Carbo 35 g; T Fat 11 g; 39% Calories from Fat; Chol 31 mg; Fiber 1 g; Sod 228 mg; Vit A 403 RE; Vit C 1 mg; Ca 67 mg; Iron 1 mg

Robert E. Lee

NORTHERN VIRGINIA CONNECTIONS

An Old Receipt for Elizabeth Monroe's Tomatoes and Eggs

Grease muffin tins; put one thick slice of unpeeled tomato into each tin; place an egg on each tomato slice; season with salt and pepper; put a small piece of butter on top. Bake in an oven until egg is set. Serve on rounds of toast and garnish with parsley. Grated cheese may be melted on top.

Some years ago a North Carolina Charlottean inherited her aunt's cookbooks; among these she found one of great interest—*Martha Washington's Rules For Cooking*. This cookbook contained recipes from four of the First Families—Washington, Jefferson, Monroe, and Madison.

Around 1797, George Washington sat down to a table of steaming crab pie, savory mutton chops, and artichokes. Thomas Jefferson's guests probably sampled the latest wines and the newest batch of spiced salad, along with other salads, hearty soups, and fresh vegetables out of Jefferson's extensive garden. Mrs. Monroe (1826) served President Monroe pate de foie gras, fried eggplant, and apple pandowdy. Dolly Madison contributed a recipe for Crab Omelet. Hand-copied recipes were shared by these families through correspondence in Virginia. The housewives took great care in exchanging recipes, much as friends do today.

GRAINS, PASTA AND VEGETARIAN DISHES

American Eating Patterns

The original eating patterns of the settlers in Virginia began nearly
four hundred years ago with the Colonial period (1600–1766). The colonists
created our first cuisine by combining the native foods with those from England,
learning food production, food preservation, and food cookery from the Indians,
and later Afro-Americans. From the Indians they learned to incorporate corn in their
cooking. Also, immigrants from every corner of the world brought many significant
culinary changes. Northern Virginians have played an important role in Americans'
food habits. They have been involved in the research that has made the technological
changes possible for improvement in foods and in nutrition. A big change began in
the early twentieth century with the advent of following a vegetarian diet and
the consumption of soy products. Today many have joined this practice
for health reasons and for enjoyment.

Vegetarian Chili

1 package Fantastic Chili Mix
1 green bell pepper, chopped
1 onion, chopped
1 garlic clove, minced
Olive oil
2 cups canned black beans
2 cups canned tomatoes
1 cup tomato sauce

Prepare the chili mix using package directions. Sauté the green pepper, onion,
and garlic in olive oil in a skillet until the vegetables are tender. Add to the chili mix.
Stir in the beans, tomatoes and tomato sauce. Simmer for 10 to 15 minutes or until
of the desired consistency, stirring occasionally.

Soy Cranberry Almond Granola

1   cup dry textured
    soy protein
1   cup old-fashioned oats
½   cup honey-toasted
    wheat germ

½   cup sliced almonds
⅓   cup honey
1   cup dried cranberries

Combine the textured soy protein, oats, wheat germ, almonds and honey in a bowl and mix well. Spread evenly in a 9x13-inch baking pan sprayed with nonstick cooking spray. Bake at 300 degrees for 10 minutes or until golden brown and slightly sticky, stirring once or twice. Stir in the cranberries.

Let stand until cool. Bake a little longer if the granola is sticky after cooling. Break the mixture into clumps. Store in an airtight container. *Yield: 8 (½-cup) servings.*

Approx Per Serving: Cal 266; Prot 18 g; Carbo 43 g; T Fat 5 g; 15% Calories from Fat; Chol 0 mg; Fiber 8 g; Sod 4 mg; Vit A 1 RE; Vit C 1 mg; Ca 106 mg; Iron 4 mg

Current research indicates that the soy protein isoflavones called daidzein and genistein may reduce the risk of osteoporosis by preventing bone loss and the breakdown of bones. In addition, soy protein helps conserve calcium in the body. While more research in this area is needed, a recent study found that forty grams of soy protein a day (two to five servings of fortified soy milk) increased bone density in the lumbar spine region of postmenopausal women.

TABOULI

A staple in the Middle East, bulgur wheat consists of wheat kernels that have been steamed, dried, and crushed into various degrees of coarseness. Bulgur has a nutlike flavor and a tender chewy texture and is used in salads and meat and vegetables dishes. Bulgur is not the same as cracked wheat.

3	cups boiling water
1	cup bulgur
1	(15-ounce) can chick-peas, drained
3	garlic cloves, minced
1	small onion, chopped
1	green bell pepper, chopped
1	red bell pepper, chopped
1	carrot, chopped

1/4	cup minced fresh mint
1/4	cup chopped fresh parsley
2	tablespoons olive oil
2	tablespoons fresh lemon juice
1	teaspoon oregano
1	teaspoon salt
1/4	teaspoon freshly ground pepper

Pour the boiling water over the bulgur in a heatproof bowl and mix well. Let stand for 1 hour or until fluffy; drain. Stir in the chick-peas, garlic, onion, bell peppers, carrot, mint and parsley.

Whisk the olive oil, lemon juice, oregano, salt and pepper in a bowl. Add to the bulgur mixture and mix well. Chill, covered, for 1 hour or longer. *Yield: 10 (1/2-cup) servings.*

Approx Per Serving: Cal 137; Prot 4 g; Carbo 24 g; T Fat 3 g; 22% Calories from Fat; Chol 0 mg; Fiber 5 g; Sod 366 mg; Vit A 287 RE; Vit C 40 mg; Ca 28 mg; Iron 1 mg

CINNAMON RICE AND LENTILS

¼	cup golden raisins	1½	cups vegetable broth
¼	cup orange juice	1	cinnamon stick
½	cup dried lentils	½	cup brown rice

Plump the raisins in the orange juice in a bowl. Sort and rinse the lentils. Bring the broth and cinnamon stick to a boil in a saucepan. Stir in the raisins, lentils and brown rice.

Bring the rice mixture to a boil; reduce heat. Simmer, covered, for 35 minutes. Discard the cinnamon stick. *Yield: 2 (1-cup) servings.*

Approx Per Serving: Cal 400; Prot 17 g; Carbo 81 g; T Fat 3 g; 6% Calories from Fat; Chol 0 mg; Fiber 12 g; Sod 758 mg; Vit A 23 RE; Vit C 18 mg; Ca 47 mg; Iron 5 mg

All rice starts as brown rice. Unlike refined white rice, brown rice is a whole grain that still contains the bran, germ, and endosperm parts of the grain. When whole grains of any kind are refined, the bran and germ are removed, taking away fiber and much of the iron, B vitamins, and other nutrients. The remaining endosperm has fewer nutrients, unless it is enriched with B vitamins and iron. Fiber cannot be replaced.

Increase the fiber in your diet by using high-fiber cereals as a coating for fish and chicken. Top fruit salads, yogurt, and ice cream with shredded bran, wheat, or other high-fiber cereals. Add bran to pancake and waffle mixes, meat loaves, soups, and ground meats. Make sandwiches on a variety of whole-grain breads.

WILD RICE AND BULGUR SALAD

Lemon Vinaigrette

¼ cup lemon juice	¼ cup olive oil
2 garlic cloves, minced	• Pepper to taste
½ teaspoon salt	

Salad

¾ cup bulgur	2 large tomatoes, chopped
6 cups hot water	1 cup chopped fresh parsley
1½ cups chicken stock	¼ cup finely chopped
¾ cup wild rice, rinsed, drained	green onions

For the vinaigrette, combine the lemon juice, garlic and salt in a food processor container. Process until blended. Add the olive oil gradually, processing constantly until smooth. Season with pepper.

For the salad, combine the bulgur and hot water in a bowl and mix well. Let stand for 1 hour; drain. Combine the stock and wild rice in a saucepan and mix well. Bring to a boil; reduce heat. Simmer, covered, for 1 hour or until the rice is tender but firm and most of the liquid is absorbed; drain. Let stand until cool. Combine the bulgur, wild rice, tomatoes, parsley and green onions in a bowl and mix well. Add the vinaigrette and toss to coat. Chill, covered, until serving time. You may store, covered, in the refrigerator for up to 2 days. *Yield: 10 (½-cup) servings.*

Approx Per Serving: Cal 141; Prot 4 g; Carbo 20 g; T Fat 6 g; 36% Calories from Fat; Chol <1 mg; Fiber 3 g; Sod 229 mg; Vit A 55 RE; Vit C 18 mg; Ca 21 mg; Iron 1 mg

RICE AND SPINACH BAKE

1	(10-ounce) package frozen cut leaf spinach	1	cup rice, cooked
1	cup milk	1	cup shredded Cheddar cheese
2	eggs, beaten	•	Salt and pepper to taste

Cook the spinach using package directions; drain. Press the spinach to remove the excess moisture. Whisk the milk and eggs in a bowl until blended. Stir in the rice and cheese. Add the spinach, salt and pepper and mix well.

Spoon the rice mixture into a 1½-quart baking dish. Bake at 350 degrees for 25 to 30 minutes or until bubbly. *Yield: 6 servings.*

Approx Per Serving: Cal 250; Prot 12 g; Carbo 29 g; T Fat 10 g; 35% Calories from Fat; Chol 96 mg; Fiber 2 g; Sod 194 mg; Vit A 464 RE; Vit C 12 mg; Ca 254 mg; Iron 3 mg

Everyone of all ages needs at least two servings of milk foods daily. Milk foods are the most concentrated source of calcium and the best utilized by the body. If you do not use milk foods, you are likely getting less than 25 percent of your daily calcium recommendation. Dark greens are often listed as the "next best" sources of calcium. However, several servings are needed to equal the calcium in one cup of milk. Soy products such as tofu or soybeans provide steady amounts of calcium. Soy milk has little calcium unless enriched. Add dried milk powder to recipes for sauces, soups, bread, puddings, casseroles, and custards to increase calcium.

Couscous is not a grain, but a form of pasta. Couscous is traditionally made from ground millet and is the pasta of northern Africa. In the United States, it is made from ground semolina wheat, and often used in salads, mixed with fruit, and in other grain dishes. Couscous is a good source of B vitamins.

MEDITERRANEAN COUSCOUS SALAD

Orange Salad Dressing

¼   cup orange juice

1   tablespoon vegetable oil

•   Grated zest of 1 orange

Salad

1   (14-ounce) can vegetable broth or water

1   cup couscous

1   (10-ounce) can chick-peas, drained

1   cup sliced scallions with green tops

½   cup raisins, dried cranberries or chopped dried apricots

¼   cup chopped fresh parsley

¼   cup crumbled feta cheese

For the dressing, whisk the orange juice, oil and zest in a bowl.

For the salad, bring the broth to a boil in a medium saucepan. Stir in the couscous. Remove from heat. Let stand, covered, for 5 minutes. Transfer the couscous to a bowl and fluff with a fork.

Add the chick-peas, scallions, raisins and parsley to the couscous and mix gently. Add the dressing and toss to coat. Spinkle with the feta cheese just before serving. *Yield: 8 (½-cup) servings.*

Approx Per Serving: Cal 192; Prot 6 g; Carbo 35 g; T Fat 4 g; 16% Calories from Fat; Chol 4 mg; Fiber 4 g; Sod 376 mg; Vit A 28 RE; Vit C 12 mg; Ca 59 mg; Iron 1 mg

LINGUINI SALAD

16 ounces linguini
1 large tomato, chopped
1 large onion, chopped
1 green bell pepper,
   chopped
1 cucumber, peeled,
   chopped

1 (16-ounce) bottle nonfat
   Italian salad dressing
½ (3-ounce) jar Salad
   Supreme seasoning

Cook the pasta in boiling water in a saucepan for 10 to 12 minutes or until al dente. Drain and rinse with cold water.

Combine the pasta, tomato, onion, bell pepper and cucumber in a bowl and mix well. Add the salad dressing and seasoning and toss to mix. The flavor of the salad is enhanced if chilled for 8 to 10 hours before serving. For variety, add sliced pepperoni, chopped cooked chicken, chopped ham, tuna or chopped eggs. *Yield: 12 servings.*

Approx Per Serving: Cal 135; Prot 6 g; Carbo 27 g; T Fat 1 g; 9% Calories from Fat; Chol 0 mg; Fiber 2 g; Sod 585 mg; Vit A 17 RE; Vit C 13 mg; Ca 6 mg; Iron 1 mg

Sesame Dressing

For variety, try Sesame Dressing on your next pasta salad. Process 1½ cups vegetable oil, 1 cup chopped fresh parsley (optional), ¼ cup toasted sesame seeds, 2 tablespoons lemon juice and ½ teaspoon salt in a blender until almost smooth. Store, covered, in the refrigerator. Yield: ½ to ¾ cup.

The Mediterranean diet is defined as a diet with an abundance of whole grains, fresh vegetables, fruits, legumes, and nuts with low to moderate use of cheese and yogurt. Olive oil is the main fat that is featured. The diet is associated with a lower incidence of heart disease.

Vegetarian Pasta Salad

8	ounces small shell pasta	½	small purple onion, thinly sliced
1	(6-ounce) jar marinated artichoke hearts, drained, coarsely chopped	½	cup freshly grated Parmesan cheese
1	(4-ounce) can sliced black olives, drained	½	cup Italian salad dressing
1	cup frozen small green peas, thawed, drained	½	cup mayonnaise
1	red bell pepper, chopped	1	teaspoon parsley flakes
1	small zucchini, chopped	½	teaspoon freshly ground pepper
		½	teaspoon dillweed

Cook the pasta using package directions without added fat or salt. Drain and rinse with cold water. Combine the artichokes, black olives, peas, bell pepper, zucchini, onion and Parmesan cheese in a bowl and mix well. Stir in the pasta.

Combine the salad dressing, mayonnaise, parsley flakes, pepper and dillweed in a bowl and mix well. Add to the pasta mixture and toss to coat. Chill, covered, until serving time. *Yield: 8 servings.*

Approx Per Serving: Cal 353; Prot 8 g; Carbo 29 g; T Fat 24 g; 59% Calories from Fat; Chol 15 mg; Fiber 4 g; Sod 514 mg; Vit A 124 RE; Vit C 34 mg; Ca 115 mg; Iron 2 mg

PINEAPPLE CHICKEN PASTA

8	ounces rotini or rotelle	¼	cup chopped green onions
1	(8-ounce) can juice-pack pineapple chunks	1	cup reduced-fat mayonnaise
1	cup seedless green grapes, cut into halves	⅛	teaspoon salt
½	cup chopped celery	⅛	teaspoon pepper
½	cup chopped green bell pepper	4	boneless skinless chicken breasts, cooked, chopped

Cook the pasta using package directions without added fat or salt; drain. Let stand until cool. Drain the pineapple, reserving 2 tablespoons of the juice.

Combine the pineapple, grapes, celery, bell pepper and green onions in a bowl and mix well. Whisk the reserved pineapple juice, mayonnaise, salt and pepper in a bowl until blended. Add to the pineapple mixture and mix gently. Stir in the pasta and chicken. Chill, covered, for 1 hour or longer before serving. *Yield: 8 servings.*

Approx Per Serving: Cal 344; Prot 30 g; Carbo 34 g; T Fat 9 g; 25% Calories from Fat; Chol 80 mg; Fiber 2 g; Sod 258 mg; Vit A 15 RE; Vit C 14 mg; Ca 30 mg; Iron 2 mg

Here are a few simple hints on ways to decrease the dietary fat and cholesterol in your diet. Choose high-fiber cereals, toast, bagels and English muffins with fruit and skim or 1% milk instead of eggs for breakfast. Include no more than three to four egg yolks per week in your diet; do not forget to count those used in cooking and baking. Eat egg whites freely. Read labels to identify fat content and the type of fat in the foods you purchase. Eat more whole grain breads and cereals. Select skim or 1% fat dairy products. Choose broiled, grilled, roasted, barbecued, and baked entrées instead of fried. Season vegetables, potatoes, rice, and noodles with herbs and spices, instead of butter or margarine.

Substitute nonfat or reduced-fat mayonnaise or plain nonfat yogurt for regular mayonnaise.

TIDEWATER SHRIMP SALAD

Recipe furnished by Belle Kuisine of Richmond, Virginia.

16	ounces small shell pasta	2	tablespoons capers
2	pounds frozen salad shrimp, thawed, drained	1	tablespoon lemon juice
		1	tablespoon celery seeds
1	cup chopped celery	¼	teaspoon salt
6	green onions, chopped	¼	teaspoon pepper
1	cup mayonnaise	¼	teaspoon Old Bay seasoning
½	cup Russian salad dressing		

Cook the pasta using package directions without added fat or salt until al dente; drain. Combine the shrimp, celery and green onions in a bowl and mix well. Combine the mayonnaise, salad dressing, capers, lemon juice, celery seeds, salt, pepper and Old Bay seasoning in a bowl and mix well. Add the mayonnaise mixture to the shrimp mixture and toss to coat. Stir in the pasta. Chill, covered, until serving time. *Yield: 20 servings.*

Approx Per Serving: Cal 222; Prot 9 g; Carbo 19 g; T Fat 13 g; 51% Calories from Fat; Chol 76 mg; Fiber 1 g; Sod 328 mg; Vit A 15 RE; Vit C 2 mg; Ca 17 mg; Iron 1 mg

GRAINS, PASTA AND VEGETARIAN DISHES

BEEF SATAY WITH PASTA

1¼	pounds boneless beef tip sirloin steak, 1 inch thick	1	tablespoon water
5	tablespoons teriyaki sauce	¼	teaspoon crushed red pepper
6	ounces vermicelli	¼	teaspoon ginger
2	tablespoons creamy peanut butter	2	tablespoons vegetable oil
		½	cup chopped seeded cucumber

Limit your intake of peanut butter to two to three tablespoons per week. Peanut butter is cholesterol-free, but very high in all fats. Seventy-five percent of the calories are from fat.

Cut the steak lengthwise into halves. Cut each half crosswise into ⅛-inch slices. Combine 2 tablespoons of the teriyaki sauce and the beef in a bowl and toss to coat. Cook the pasta using package directions without added fat or salt; drain. Cover to keep warm.

Combine the remaining 3 tablespoons teriyaki sauce, peanut butter, water, red pepper and ginger in a bowl and mix well. Add the pasta and mix well. Cover to keep warm.

Heat the oil in a large nonstick skillet or wok over medium heat until hot. Add the beef ½ at a time. Stir-fry for 1 to 2 minutes or until no longer pink; do not overcook. Add the beef to the pasta mixture and toss to mix. Sprinkle with the cucumber. Serve immediately. *Yield: 4 servings.*

Approx Per Serving: Cal 500; Prot 41 g; Carbo 39 g; T Fat 19 g; 35% Calories from Fat; Chol 93 mg; Fiber 3 g; Sod 971 mg; Vit A 1 RE; Vit C <1 mg; Ca 31 mg; Iron 6 mg

BOLOGNESE PASTA SAUCE

1	pound ground turkey or ground round	1½	cups red wine or dry white wine
1	large onion, chopped	2	tablespoons parsley flakes
1	medium carrot, chopped	1	teaspoon sugar
1	rib celery, chopped	•	Salt and pepper to taste
3	garlic cloves, minced	16	ounces rigatoni, penne or fettuccini, cooked, drained
2	tablespoons olive oil		
2	(16-ounce) cans crushed tomatoes	½	cup grated Parmesan cheese
2	cups beef stock		

Sauté the ground turkey with the onion, carrot, celery and garlic in the olive oil in a skillet over low heat for 5 minutes; drain. Add the undrained tomatoes, stock, red wine, parsley flakes and sugar and mix well. Bring to a boil; reduce heat.

Simmer for 1½ hours, stirring occasionally. Season with salt and pepper. Spoon over the pasta on a serving platter. Sprinkle with the cheese. *Yield: 8 servings.*

Approx Per Serving: Cal 448; Prot 24 g; Carbo 54 g; T Fat 13 g; 25% Calories from Fat; Chol 49 mg; Fiber 5 g; Sod 532 mg; Vit A 349 RE; Vit C 14 mg; Ca 165 mg; Iron 4 mg

TANTALIZING TURKEY PASTA SAUCE

5   (14-ounce) cans whole
    tomatoes
1   pound ground turkey
    breast (98% fat-free)
1   medium onion, chopped
2   to 3 (6-ounce) cans
    tomato paste
2   tomato paste cans water
3   ounces Romano cheese,
    grated
1/3 cup sugar

2   tablespoons oregano
1   to 2 tablespoons
    garlic powder
1   tablespoon basil
1   tablespoon Italian
    seasoning
1   tablespoon Worcestershire
    sauce
1½ teaspoons salt
•   Pepper to taste

Process the tomatoes in a food processor until puréed. Brown the turkey with the onion in a skillet, stirring until the ground turkey is crumbly; drain. Transfer the turkey mixture to a large saucepan.

Add the puréed tomatoes, tomato paste, water, cheese, sugar, oregano, garlic powder, basil, Italian seasoning, Worcestershire sauce, salt and pepper to the turkey mixture and mix well. Simmer, covered, for 2 hours or until of the desired consistency, stirring occasionally.

Spoon the pasta sauce over your favorite hot cooked pasta on a serving platter. You may freeze the sauce for future use. *Yield: 10 (1-cup) servings.*

Approx Per Serving: Cal 192; Prot 17 g; Carbo 28 g; T Fat 3 g; 14% Calories from Fat; Chol 29 mg; Fiber 5 g; Sod 1140 mg; Vit A 249 RE; Vit C 48 mg; Ca 189 mg; Iron 3 mg

Be sure to read labels to find "hidden" sodium in foods and medications. Look for the symbol "Na" and for the words salt, sodium, soda, brine, monosodium glutamate and sodium bicarbonate. A low-sodium food should provide 140 milligrams or less per serving. Low sodium frozen dinners are higher if they are full meals, with milligram amounts ranging in the 500s to 600s.

SHRIMP AND CLAM LINGUINI

Typically, this dish is prepared with Alfredo Sauce, a high-fat cream sauce. This is Virginia's best, demonstrating a gourmet alternative for a heart-healthy lifestyle.

6	ounces linguini	8	ounces mushrooms, sliced
½	cup (1 stick) margarine or butter	½	cup grated Parmesan cheese
2	garlic cloves, minced	1	(14-ounce) can red clam sauce
1	teaspoon oregano		
8	ounces deveined peeled shrimp		

Cook the pasta using package directions without added fat or salt until al dente; drain. Heat the margarine in a saucepan until melted. Stir in the garlic and oregano. Sauté the shrimp and mushrooms in the butter mixture until the shrimp turn pink. Add the cheese and mix well. Add the pasta and clam sauce and mix well.

Spoon the shrimp mixture into a baking dish sprayed with nonstick cooking spray. Bake at 325 degrees for 10 minutes or until heated through. *Yield: 6 servings.*

Approx Per Serving: Cal 330; Prot 17 g; Carbo 22 g; T Fat 20 g; 54% Calories from Fat; Chol 63 mg; Fiber 2 g; Sod 773 mg; Vit A 204 RE; Vit C 1 mg; Ca 143 mg; Iron 2 mg

Spinach Lasagna Twirls

12	lasagna noodles	1	carrot, grated
1	(16-ounce) jar spaghetti sauce	2	to 3 garlic cloves, minced
1	(10-ounce) package frozen chopped spinach, thawed, drained	1	teaspoon olive oil
		15	ounces nonfat ricotta cheese
1	(3-ounce) can mushroom bits and pieces, drained	1/4	teaspoon salt
		1/8	teaspoon pepper
1	medium onion, chopped	1/4	to 1/2 cup grated Parmesan cheese

Cook the noodles in boiling water in a large saucepan until al dente. Drain and separate the noodles to prevent them from sticking together. Spray a 9x13-inch baking pan with nonstick cooking spray. Spread enough of the spaghetti sauce over the bottom of the prepared pan to cover and set aside. Press the spinach to remove the excess moisture.

Sauté the mushrooms, onion, carrot and garlic in the olive oil in a skillet until the vegetables are tender. Stir in the spinach, ricotta cheese, salt and pepper. Lay the noodles 1 at a time on a flat surface. Spread 3 to 4 tablespoons of the spinach mixture over 1 side of each noodle. Roll to enclose the filling.

Cut each roll into halves, allowing the curly edges of the noodles to remain intact. Arrange curly edges up in the prepared baking pan. Spoon the remaining spaghetti sauce over the rolls. Sprinkle with the Parmesan cheese. Bake, covered, at 350 degrees for 25 minutes or until heated through. *Yield: 6 servings.*

Approx Per Serving: Cal 253; Prot 15 g; Carbo 33 g; T Fat 7 g; 26% Calories from Fat; Chol 7 mg; Fiber 6 g; Sod 788 mg; Vit A 812 RE; Vit C 23 mg; Ca 203 mg; Iron 2 mg

Eating twenty-five to fifty grams of soy protein per day may be enough to lower cholesterol. Two servings (1/2 cup per serving) of firm tofu provide almost forty grams of soy protein.

VEGETARIAN LASAGNA

1 cup sliced mushrooms	1½ cups cottage cheese
½ cup minced onion	8 ounces cream cheese, softened
3 garlic cloves, minced	• Salt and pepper to taste
2 teaspoons basil	16 ounces lasagna noodles, cooked, drained
1 cup sliced carrots	
1 cup sliced zucchini	8 ounces mozzarella cheese, shredded
1 cup chopped red bell pepper	
1 cup broccoli florets, chopped	¾ cup grated Parmesan cheese
2 cups ricotta cheese	

Sauté the mushrooms, onion, garlic and basil in a nonstick skillet until the onion is tender. Steam the carrots, zucchini, bell pepper and broccoli until tender. Combine the ricotta cheese, cottage cheese and cream cheese in a mixing bowl. Beat at low speed until blended. Stir in the sautéed and steamed vegetables. Season with salt and pepper.

Line the bottom of a 9x13-inch baking dish with ⅓ of the noodles. Spread with ½ of the ricotta cheese mixture, ⅓ of the mozzarella cheese and ⅓ of the Parmesan cheese. Top with ½ of the remaining noodles, the remaining ricotta cheese mixture, ½ of the remaining mozzarella cheese and ½ of the remaining Parmesan cheese. Layer with the remaining noodles, remaining mozzarella cheese and remaining Parmesan cheese. Bake at 375 degrees for 50 minutes. Let stand for 10 minutes before serving. *Yield: 8 servings.*

Approx Per Serving: Cal 481; Prot 27 g; Carbo 28 g; T Fat 29 g; 54% Calories from Fat; Chol 98 mg; Fiber 2 g; Sod 586 mg; Vit A 861 RE; Vit C 50 mg; Ca 477 mg; Iron 2 mg

Rigatoni, Broccoli and Mozzarella Melt

- **Florets of 1 bunch broccoli**
- 2 **tablespoons olive oil**
- 12 **ounces small rigatoni**
- 2 **garlic cloves, crushed**
- ¼ **cup (½ stick) butter or margarine**
- ¼ **cup flour**
- 2 **cups milk**
- ½ **teaspoon salt**
- 3 **cups shredded mozzarella cheese**

Combine the broccoli with enough water to cover in a saucepan. Cook for 2 minutes or until tender-crisp; drain. Rinse with cold water; drain. Return the broccoli to the saucepan. Add 1 tablespoon of the olive oil and toss to coat.

Cook the pasta using package directions until al dente; drain. Rinse with cold water; drain. Return the pasta to the saucepan. Add the remaining 1 tablespoon olive oil and toss to coat.

Sauté the garlic in the butter in a saucepan until tender. Stir in the flour. Cook until smooth and bubbly, stirring constantly. Add the milk gradually, stirring constantly. Cook until thickened, stirring constantly. Stir in the salt. Remove from heat. Stir in the pasta.

Layer ½ of the pasta mixture, broccoli and ½ of the cheese in a 9x13-inch baking pan sprayed with nonstick cooking spray. Top with the remaining pasta mixture and remaining cheese. Bake, covered with foil, at 350 degrees for 25 to 30 minutes; remove the foil. Bake for 10 minutes longer. You may substitute two 10-ounce packages thawed frozen broccoli for the fresh broccoli. *Yield: 8 servings.*

Approx Per Serving: Cal 410; Prot 17 g; Carbo 39 g; T Fat 21 g; 46% Calories from Fat; Chol 57 mg; Fiber 2 g; Sod 399 mg; Vit A 228 RE; Vit C 17 mg; Ca 313 mg; Iron 2 mg

The isoflavones found in soybeans appear to have positive health benefits. Although soy foods differ somewhat in their concentration of isoflavones, all of the traditional soy foods such as soy milk, soy flour, tofu, tempeh, and soybeans are rich sources.

SZECHUAN NOODLES

16	ounces thin noodles, spaghetti or linguini	2	teaspoons hot bean paste
5	tablespoons soy sauce	$1^{1/2}$	teaspoons sugar
$2^{1/2}$	tablespoons tahini	1	teaspoon minced gingerroot
1	tablespoon toasted sesame seeds (optional)	2	green onions, minced
1	tablespoon sesame oil	2	garlic cloves, minced
1	tablespoon Chinese rice vinegar		

Cook the pasta using package directions without added fat or salt until al dente; drain. Cover to keep warm. Combine the soy sauce, tahini, sesame seeds, sesame oil, rice vinegar, bean paste, sugar and gingerroot in a bowl and mix well. Stir in the green onions and garlic. Add the pasta to the soy sauce mixture and toss to coat. For variety, add steamed shrimp or chopped cooked chicken. *Yield: 8 servings.*

Approx Per Serving: Cal 269; Prot 9 g; Carbo 46 g; T Fat 5 g; 18% Calories from Fat; Chol 0 mg; Fiber 2 g; Sod 829 mg; Vit A 1 RE; Vit C 1 mg; Ca 21 mg; Iron 2 mg

Black Bean Burritos

1	(15-ounce) can black beans, drained, rinsed	4	ounces Monterey Jack cheese, shredded
2	cups cooked brown rice	20	whole wheat tortillas
1	cup medium-hot salsa		

Combine the beans, brown rice, salsa and cheese in a bowl and mix well. Microwave the tortillas 5 at a time for 1 minute or until warm. Spoon 2 tablespoons of the black bean mixture on 1 side of each tortilla. Fold over the filling, fold in the sides and roll.

Arrange the burritos seam side down on a microwave-safe dish. Microwave for 1 minute or until heated through. May warm in a 325-degree oven for 15 minutes. Serve with additional salsa, yogurt cheese and/or reduced-fat sour cream. *Yield: 20 burritos.*

Approx Per Burrito: Cal 136; Prot 6 g; Carbo 28 g; T Fat 3 g; 14% Calories from Fat; Chol 5 mg; Fiber 4 g; Sod 324 mg; Vit A 22 RE; Vit C 2 mg; Ca 65 mg; Iron 1 mg

Decrease calories, total fat, saturated fat, and cholesterol in your diet with these substitutions. Substitute soybean oil margarine for lard, butter, or shortening. Substitute 3/4 tablespoon soybean oil for 1 tablespoon non-soy margarine, 3/4 cup soybean oil for 1 cup non-soy margarine, or 1/3 cup soybean oil for 1/2 cup non-soy margarine. Substitute a mixture of 3 tablespoons baking cocoa and 1 tablespoon soybean oil for 1 ounce baking chocolate. Substitute 1 cup fortified soy milk for 1 cup whole dairy milk. Substitute a mixture of 1 tablespoon soy flour and 1 tablespoon water or one 2-inch square of tofu for 1 egg. Substitute 1 tablespoon soy flour for 2 tablespoons all-purpose flour.

SAFFRON BEANS AND CHEESE CASSOULET

1	(7-ounce) package yellow saffron rice	3	cups chopped lettuce
2	(14-ounce) cans black beans	2	cups chopped tomatoes
¼	cup chopped green onions	3	cups shredded sharp Cheddar cheese
		1	(16-ounce) jar salsa

Cook the rice using package directions without added fat or salt. Bring the undrained beans to a boil in a saucepan; drain.

Layer the saffron rice, beans, green onions, lettuce, tomatoes, cheese and salsa in the order listed in a 9x13-inch dish. Serve immediately with tortilla chips and/or crackers. *Yield: 8 servings.*

Approx Per Serving: Cal 359; Prot 19 g; Carbo 39 g; T Fat 15 g; 37% Calories from Fat; Chol 44 mg; Fiber 8 g; Sod 1245 mg; Vit A 188 RE; Vit C 19 mg; Ca 379 mg; Iron 4 mg

Easy Bean Chili

Here is a chili recipe full of fiber, low in fat, and easily prepared in approximately forty-five minutes. The secret is using canned beans and seasoned tomatoes. If you prefer chili with meat, add eight ounces browned lean ground beef.

Take a cup of dry textured vegetable protein and cover with water that is boiling or at room temperature. Let stand for 5 minutes or until plump. Combine the moist textured vegetable protein with ground beef or ground turkey or use by itself to make your favorite meat loaf, taco filling, meatballs, stuffed cabbage, stuffed bell peppers, sloppy Joes, or chili.

1	teaspoon vegetable oil (optional)	1	(14-ounce) can Mexican-style stewed tomatoes
1	cup chopped onion	1	(10-ounce) package frozen butter beans or lima beans, thawed
1	medium green bell pepper, chopped		
2	large garlic cloves, chopped	1	cup salsa
1	(15-ounce) can pinto beans, drained, rinsed	3	tablespoons chili powder, or to taste
1	(15-ounce) can kidney beans, drained, rinsed	1	tablespoon cumin
		1	tablespoon oregano
1	(15-ounce) can white beans or garbanzos, drained, rinsed	1	teaspoon red wine vinegar
		•	Cayenne pepper to taste
		•	Red wine vinegar to taste

Coat a large saucepan with nonstick cooking spray or with the oil. Heat until hot. Sauté the onion, bell pepper and garlic in the saucepan until the vegetables are tender. Add the pinto beans, kidney beans, white beans, undrained tomatoes, butter beans, salsa, chili powder, cumin, oregano and 1 teaspoon wine vinegar and mix well. Bring to a boil; reduce heat.

Simmer, covered, for 30 minutes or until the flavors have blended and the lima beans are tender, stirring occasionally. Season with cayenne pepper and additional wine vinegar. Ladle into chili bowls. Serve with your favorite toppings.

You may prepare the chili up to 2 days in advance and store, covered, in the refrigerator. Reheat over low heat. *Yield: 8 servings.*

Approx Per Serving: Cal 250; Prot 14 g; Carbo 47 g; T Fat 2 g; 6% Calories from Fat; Chol 0 mg; Fiber 12 g; Sod 622 mg; Vit A 152 RE; Vit C 26 mg; Ca 145 mg; Iron 6 mg

The following soy foods contain the greatest amount of isoflavones, providing a range of thirty to fifty milligrams per serving: 1 ounce roasted soy nuts, ½ cup soy flour, ¼ cup soy grits, ½ cup cooked textured soy protein, ½ cup cooked soybeans, 1 cup soy milk, ½ cup tempeh, and ½ cup tofu.

FALAFEL

Patties

1	pound dried chick-peas or garbanzos	½	teaspoon pepper
1	large onion, finely chopped	½	teaspoon salt
1	bunch parsley, finely chopped	¼	teaspoon cumin, or ½ teaspoon Middle Eastern spices
2	garlic cloves, minced	¼	teaspoon baking soda
		•	Peanut oil for frying

Tahini Sauce

¼	cup chopped fresh parsley	⅛	teaspoon salt
¼	cup tahini	½	cup (or more) water
2	tablespoons lemon juice		

4	(6-inch) pita rounds, cut into halves	1	cucumber, peeled, chopped
•	Chopped lettuce to taste	1	large tomato, chopped

For the patties, sort and rinse the chick-peas. Combine the chick-peas in a bowl with enough water to cover generously. Let stand for 8 to 10 hours. Drain and rinse the chick-peas. Process the chick-peas in a blender until ground. Combine the ground chick-peas, onion, parsley and garlic in a bowl and mix well. Stir in the pepper, salt, cumin and baking soda. Shape the mixture into eight 1½-inch patties. Fry in the peanut oil in a skillet for 3 to 4 minutes or until golden brown on both sides, turning once; drain.

For the sauce, process the parsley, tahini, lemon juice and salt in a blender until smooth. Add the water 1 tablespoon at a time, processing constantly until the sauce is of the desired consistency.

To assemble, arrange 1 patty in each pita pocket. Top with lettuce, cucumber and tomato. Spoon 1 tablespoon of the sauce over the top.
Yield: 8 servings.

Approx Per Serving: Cal 340; Prot 15 g; Carbo 54 g; T Fat 8 g; 21% Calories from Fat; Chol 0 mg; Fiber 11 g; Sod 400 mg; Vit A 68 RE; Vit C 22 mg; Ca 114 mg; Iron 5 mg
Nutritional information does not include peanut oil for frying.

Vegetable Jambalaya

1 cup chopped onion	1 cup cooked black-eyed peas
½ cup chopped carrot	3½ cups water, vegetable broth or chicken broth
¼ cup chopped celery	
2 garlic cloves, minced	1 (16-ounce) can chopped tomatoes
2 teaspoons paprika	
1 teaspoon thyme	1¼ cups long grain rice
½ teaspoon salt (optional)	1 zucchini, chopped
⅛ teaspoon cayenne pepper	½ cup chopped fresh parsley
1 bay leaf	½ cup grated Parmesan cheese
2 green bell peppers, chopped	
2 red bell peppers, chopped	

Heat a large saucepan over medium heat until hot. Spray with nonstick cooking spray. Add the onion, carrot, celery and garlic. Cook for several minutes or until the vegetables are tender, stirring frequently. Stir in the paprika, thyme, salt, cayenne pepper and bay leaf. Add the bell peppers, black-eyed peas, water and undrained tomatoes.

Bring to a boil, stirring occasionally. Stir in the rice and zucchini. Reduce the heat to low. Simmer, covered, for 20 minutes or until the rice is tender, stirring occasionally. Discard the bay leaf. Sprinkle with the parsley and cheese just before serving. *Yield: 6 servings.*

Approx Per Serving: Cal 272; Prot 11 g; Carbo 50 g; T Fat 3 g; 11% Calories from Fat; Chol 7 mg; Fiber 6 g; Sod 302 mg; Vit A 635 RE; Vit C 133 mg; Ca 176 mg; Iron 4 mg

Antioxidants are thought to interfere with the aging and disease process by neutralizing harmful molecules in our bodies called free radicals. The data supporting this idea is not conclusive as some studies show evidence of anti-oxidants helping out the disease process and others do not give as much proof. The jury is still out, but the future looks promising for antioxidants. Three antioxidant vitamins that appear to play a unique role by neutralizing free radicals are vitamin A, vitamin C, and vitamin E. Some enzymes that have trace minerals such as selenium, copper, zinc, and manganese also act as antioxidants.

Weight loss appears to be associated with bone loss. Exercise is important in helping maintain bone mineral density.

RATATOUILLE

½ cup chopped onion
2 garlic cloves, minced
1 teaspoon olive oil
2 cups chopped eggplant
1 green bell pepper, chopped
1 red bell pepper, chopped
1 medium zucchini, chopped
1 cup sliced fresh mushrooms
1 (8-ounce) can diced stewed tomatoes
¼ cup chopped fresh basil
2 tablespoons dry white wine
• Salt and pepper to taste
8 ounces penne, cooked, drained
¼ cup finely grated Parmesan cheese

Sauté the onion and garlic in the olive oil in a large saucepan until the onion is tender. Stir in the eggplant, bell peppers, zucchini, mushrooms, undrained tomatoes, basil and white wine.

Sauté for 20 minutes or until the vegetables are tender. Season with salt and pepper. Spoon over hot cooked pasta on a serving platter. Sprinkle with the cheese. *Yield: 4 servings.*

Approx Per Serving: Cal 324; Prot 12 g; Carbo 58 g; T Fat 4 g; 12% Calories from Fat; Chol 5 mg; Fiber 5 g; Sod 238 mg; Vit A 243 RE; Vit C 95 mg; Ca 132 mg; Iron 1 mg

Natural Bridge

FLAVORS OF THE COMMONWEALTH

To Dry Herbs

Gather them on a dry day, just before they begin to blossom, brush off the dust, cut them in small branches, and dry them quickly in a moderate oven; pick off the leaves when dry, pound and sift them—bottle immediately, and cork them closely. They must be kept in a dry place.

The Virginia House-wife, 1824
Mary Randolph

Documentary sources give copious lists of herbs and vegetables grown in the seventeenth century but little information on their use. The following herbs were mentioned from this period: sorrel, marjoram, thyme, savory, houseleeks, rue, coriander, balm, basil, rosemary, dill, caraway, cumin, anise, and spearmint. Most of the American Indian tribes used native plants such as sassafras, yerba buena, and chaparral, and the settlers adopted the use of these.

BRUNCH AND MORE

The Flavors of American Cooking

Foods served in Virginia started with European and colonial regional tradition. Captain John Smith's correspondence showed there was a primitive system for eating: first survival, then learning food production and food preservation from the native Indians.

Cookbooks were not used in the 1600s due to lack of the English ingredients and the new foods found in America. As the environment developed, so did the culinary influence. In 1742, William Parks, of Williamsburg, published a cookbook that had been written by Eliza Smith of London, *The Compleat Housewife* or *Accomplished Gentlewoman's Companion*. A popular cookbook used was *The Art of Cookery Made Plain and Easy, 1789*, by Hannah Glasse of England. In the 1800s, the most-used cookbook was written by Mary Randolph, *The Virginia House-wife, 1824*. Other manuscript books were written by Thomas Jefferson, Martha Washington, and other plantation housewives. Written records by families in Virginia have given us an idea of their excursion into the culinary area.

Colorings were used for elegant desserts: beet juice for red coloring and spinach juice for green coloring. The seasonings became more important in the 19th century; nutmeg came from the Spice Islands. Herbs were grown in the kitchen gardens for flavor and for medicinal purposes.

C. F. Sauer Co. was founded in Virginia about 1887 by Mr. Sauer, a pharmacist. Today the company continues to produce herbs and spices, salad dressings, vegetable oils, mustard, peanut products, gravy, sauces, and seasoning mixes.

Flavors of Virginia reflect the culture of many ethnic groups who brought a variety of seasonings. The diversity of cultures has shaped the Virginian and the American cuisine we know today.

Colonial Game Pie

From King's Arms Tavern in Williamsburg, Virginia.

1	(4- to 5-pound) duck, dressed	½	teaspoon freshly ground pepper
•	Salt to taste	1½	pounds mushrooms, cut into quarters
2	pounds rabbit		
2	pounds venison, cut into bite-size pieces	¼	cup (½ stick) butter
½	cup vegetable oil	1	pound slab bacon, cut into 1-inch pieces, cooked
2	cups port wine		
1½	quarts basic brown sauce	1	(15-ounce) can pearl onions, heated, drained
1	cup currant jelly		
1	garlic clove, minced	•	Pie pastry
1	tablespoon Worcestershire sauce	1	egg
		2	tablespoons milk

Sprinkle the inside cavity of the duck with salt. Arrange breast side up on a rack in a roasting pan. Bake at 400 degrees for 30 minutes. Reduce the oven temperature to 325 degrees. Bake until the duck is tender. Cool slightly. Cut into bite-size pieces. Simmer the rabbit in a small amount of water in a stockpot for 1 hour or until tender. Drain and cut into bite-size pieces.

Sauté the venison in the oil in a Dutch oven until brown on all sides. Remove the venison to a platter with a slotted spoon. Drain the oil from the skillet. Add the wine to the skillet. Bring to a boil, stirring to loosen any brown particles. Boil for 2 to 3 minutes. Return the venison to the skillet. Stir in the brown sauce. Simmer for 45 to 60 minutes or until the venison is tender. Add the duck and rabbit and mix well. Stir in the currant jelly, garlic, Worcestershire sauce and pepper. Cover to keep warm.

Sauté the mushrooms in the butter in a skillet. Spoon the duck mixture into individual baking dishes. Sprinkle the mushrooms, bacon and onions over the top. Cover with pastry and prick. Brush the pastry with a mixture of the egg and milk. Bake at 350 degrees for 20 to 25 minutes or until golden brown. Serve immediately. *Yield: 12 to 15 servings.*

Nutritional information for this recipe is not available.

Lemon Bread Pudding

Arrange 1 cup bread cubes in a greased 1½-quart baking dish. Sprinkle with the grated zest of 2 large lemons. Bring 2 cups whole or skim milk and ½ cup sugar to a boil in a saucepan. Stir in 3 tablespoons butter or margarine. Pour over the bread cubes. Let stand until cool. Beat 4 egg yolks in a mixing bowl until blended. Stir in the juice of 2 large lemons. Beat 4 egg whites and ½ teaspoon salt in a mixing bowl until stiff peaks form. Fold into the lemon mixture. Spoon over the prepared layers. Sprinkle with confectioners' sugar. Place the baking dish in a larger baking pan. Add just enough hot water to reach halfway up the side of the baking dish. Bake at 350 degrees for 1 hour. Yield: 8 servings.

BLUE KNOLL CHEESY APPLE EGG BAKE

From Blue Knoll Farm Bed & Breakfast in Castleton, Virginia. The original house is pre–Civil War with an addition added at the turn of the twentieth century. Guests cross the threshold and enter the peaceful ambiance of a time almost forgotten. Hosts Mary and Gil Carlson will make every effort to spoil you in their unspoiled, tranquil setting. Many country attractions are nearby, or guests can simply sit and rock the day away on one of several lovely porches.

2	cups sliced peeled Granny Smith apples	2	cups shredded Cheddar cheese
2	tablespoons cinnamon-sugar	2	cups milk
6	slices crisp-cooked bacon, crumbled	6	eggs
		2	cups baking mix

Layer the apples, cinnamon-sugar, bacon and cheese in the order listed in a 9x13-inch baking dish sprayed with nonstick cooking spray. Whisk the milk and eggs in a bowl until blended. Add the baking mix and stir until smooth.

Pour the egg mixture over the prepared layers. Bake at 375 degrees for 40 minutes or until set. Serve with warm maple syrup. *Yield: 8 servings.*

Approx Per Serving: Cal 402; Prot 20 g; Carbo 50 g; T Fat 18 g; 37% Calories from Fat; Chol 201 mg; Fiber 3 g; Sod 648 mg; Vit A 170 RE; Vit C 2 mg; Ca 346 mg; Iron 2 mg

Jackie's Sausage Apple Quiche

From Edgewood Farm Bed & Breakfast in Standardsville, Virginia. This recipe is an example of one of the many sumptuous dishes served by your hosts, Eleanor and Norman Schwartz.

8 ounces Italian turkey sausage, cooked, drained, crumbled	1 cup shredded sharp Cheddar cheese
1½ cups chopped apples	4 eggs, beaten
½ teaspoon cinnamon	1 cup milk
½ teaspoon nutmeg	½ cup baking mix

Layer the sausage and apples in a greased 7x11-inch baking dish or 9-inch round baking dish. Sprinkle with the cinnamon, nutmeg and cheese. Pour the eggs over the prepared layers.

Combine the milk and baking mix in a bowl and mix well. Spoon over the top. Bake at 375 degrees for 30 to 40 minutes or until a knife inserted in the center comes out clean. Serve immediately. *Yield: 4 servings.*

Approx Per Serving: Cal 365; Prot 23 g; Carbo 26 g; T Fat 19 g; 46% Calories from Fat; Chol 267 mg; Fiber 2 g; Sod 603 mg; Vit A 195 RE; Vit C 2 mg; Ca 328 mg; Iron 2 mg

What does cooking mean? It means the knowledge of Medea, and of Circe, and of Calypso, and of Helen, and of Rebekah, and of the Queen of Sheba. It means the knowledge of all herbs, and fruits, and balms, and spices; and of all that is healing and sweet in fields and groves, and savory in meats; it means carefulness, and inventiveness, and watchfulness, and willingness, and readiness of appliance; it means the economy of your great-grandmothers, and the science of modern chemists; it means much tasting, and no wasting; it means English thoroughness, and French art, and Arabian hospitality.

John Ruskin
The Monticello
Cook Book, *1950*

Herbed Mock Hollandaise Sauce

Whisk 1/3 cup reduced-fat mayonnaise, 2 tablespoons water, 2 teaspoons lemon juice, 1 teaspoon chopped fresh tarragon or rosemary and 1/8 teaspoon pepper in a saucepan until mixed. Cook over low heat for 3 to 4 minutes or until heated through, stirring constantly. Serve warm. You may substitute 1/4 teaspoon dried tarragon or rosemary for the fresh herbs.

EGGS FLORENTINE 'LIGHT'

From Thornrose House Bed & Breakfast at Gypsy Hill in Staunton, Virginia. This turn-of-the-century Georgian Revival home with a wraparound verandah sits on an acre of gardens festooned with Greek colonnades. Innkeepers Suzy and Otis Huston begin breakfasts with Birchermuesli and follow with fresh baked muffins and breads and hot entrées such as the following. This recipe is a wonderful lighter version of an old favorite. It is actually a tasty combination of Eggs Benedict and Eggs Florentine . . . taking the best of both, and leaving the fat behind.

1	pound fresh spinach, trimmed	4	slices tomato
2	English muffins, split	4	eggs, poached
2	teaspoons butter, softened	1	recipe Herbed Mock Hollandaise Sauce (at left)
2	thin slices cooked turkey ham, cut into halves		

Steam the spinach until tender; drain. Cover to keep warm. Spread each muffin half with 1/2 teaspoon butter. Arrange the halves on a baking sheet. Broil until light brown.

Layer the ham, tomato slices and spinach on the muffin halves. Top each with a poached egg. Drizzle each with 2 tablespoons of the hollandaise sauce. Serve immediately. You may substitute one 10-ounce package cooked frozen leaf spinach for the fresh spinach. *Yield: 4 servings.*

Approx Per Serving: Cal 251; Prot 15 g; Carbo 22 g; T Fat 12 g; 43% Calories from Fat; Chol 231 mg; Fiber 4 g; Sod 643 mg; Vit A 888 RE; Vit C 37 mg; Ca 190 mg; Iron 5 mg
Nutritional information includes the entire amount of the Herbed Mock Hollandaise Sauce.

SMITHFIELD INN STEWED TOMATOES

Exceptionally good served with black-eyed peas.

1	(16-ounce) can stewed tomatoes	1	tablespoon butter, melted
¼	cup (or less) sugar	1	teaspoon flour
2	dry biscuits, crumbled	½	teaspoon vanilla extract
		½	teaspoon lemon extract

Mash the undrained tomatoes in a bowl. Stir in the sugar, biscuits, butter, flour and flavorings. Spoon the tomato mixture into a greased 1-quart baking dish.

Bake at 350 degrees for 30 to 40 minutes or until bubbly. May substitute 2 slices cubed dry bread for the biscuits. *Yield: 3 servings.*

Approx Per Serving: Cal 296; Prot 4 g; Carbo 46 g; T Fat 10 g; 32% Calories from Fat; Chol 12 mg; Fiber 2 g; Sod 581 mg; Vit A 82 RE; Vit C 11 mg; Ca 145 mg; Iron 2 mg

Add fresh herbs during the last twenty to thirty minutes of the cooking or baking process, except for bay leaves, which may be baked or cooked for several hours. The flavor of fresh herbs is decreased with longer cooking or baking times.

Both olive oil and canola oil are high in monounsaturated fatty acids and low in saturated fatty acids. Monounsaturated fatty acids in foods may help lower blood cholesterol levels more than polyunsaturated fatty acids do. However, simply adding olive or canola oil to an already high-fat diet is not the point. These oils are still 100 percent fat with 120 calories per tablespoon. The goal for health is to use oils high in monounsaturated fatty acids instead of other fats and oils.

Sabine's Zucchini Slice

From Edgewood Farm Bed & Breakfast in Standardsville, Virginia. The quiet seclusion of a 130-acre farm in the foothills of the Blue Ridge is the setting for the house, originally built in 1790. It has since been restored to its former glory and is run by your hosts, Eleanor and Norman Schwartz. Each guest room is decorated in furnishings of the period and includes a fireplace. The Schwartzes greet you upon arrival with refreshments, then serve a sumptuous breakfast each morning.

1	cup flour	1	cup shredded sharp Cheddar cheese
5	eggs, beaten		
¼	cup olive oil	3	slices crisp-cooked bacon, drained, crumbled
3	zucchini, grated		
1	large onion, chopped	•	Salt and pepper to taste

Whisk the flour, eggs and olive oil in a bowl until blended. Stir in the zucchini, onion, cheese and bacon. Season with salt and pepper. Spoon into a greased 7x11-inch baking dish.

Bake at 350 degrees until set or until a knife inserted in the center comes out clean. Serve warm. Omit the bacon if desired. *Yield: 6 servings.*

Approx Per Serving: Cal 334; Prot 14 g; Carbo 21 g; T Fat 21 g; 57% Calories from Fat; Chol 200 mg; Fiber 2 g; Sod 224 mg; Vit A 165 RE; Vit C 10 mg; Ca 179 mg; Iron 2 mg

CRANBERRY APPLE SCONES

From Sampson Eagon Inn in Staunton, Virginia. Innkeepers Frank and Laura Mattingly love creating unusual recipes. These scones are so moist that no butter is needed when serving.

2¼	cups unbleached flour	1	cup coarsely chopped apple
½	cup granulated sugar		
1	tablespoon (heaping) baking powder	1	cup coarsely chopped cranberries
¼	teaspoon salt	2	tablespoons whipping cream
¾	cup milk		
½	cup (1 stick) butter, melted	2	tablespoons coarse or decorating sugar
1	egg, lightly beaten		
1	teaspoon vanilla extract		

Combine the flour, ½ cup sugar, baking powder and salt in a bowl and mix well. Whisk the milk, butter, egg and vanilla in a bowl until blended. Stir in the apple. Add the apple mixture to the flour mixture and mix well. Fold in the cranberries.

Spread the batter in a greased 10-inch springform pan. Brush the top with the whipping cream and sprinkle with the coarse sugar. Bake at 350 degrees for 35 to 40 minutes or until golden brown. Serve warm. Freeze, wrapped in foil, for future use. Reheat before serving. *Yield: 8 servings.*

Approx Per Serving: Cal 343; Prot 5 g; Carbo 48 g; T Fat 15 g; 38% Calories from Fat; Chol 66 mg; Fiber 2 g; Sod 394 mg; Vit A 143 RE; Vit C 3 mg; Ca 145 mg; Iron 2 mg

Tough-stemmed herbs such as basil, tarragon, and sage should have their leaves removed before freezing. Arrange the leaves in a single layer on a baking sheet. Freeze for several hours. Store in sealable freezer bags in the freezer. Blanch basil before freezing to prevent the leaves from turning black. You may freeze sprigs of delicate herbs like dillweed and thyme for future use. Store in sealable freezer bags in the freezer.

CRESCENT CHEESE TWISTS

1	(8-count) can crescent rolls
2	teaspoons butter, melted
1	to 2 tablespoons shredded Cheddar cheese
¼	teaspoon garlic salt or onion salt

Unroll the crescent roll dough. Separate into 4 rectangles, pressing the perforations to seal. Brush 1 side of 2 of the rectangles with the butter. Sprinkle the cheese and garlic salt over the butter.

Arrange the remaining 2 rectangles over the prepared rectangles. Cut each crosswise into ten ½-inch strips. Twist each strip 5 or 6 times and arrange on an ungreased baking sheet, securing the ends by pressing to the baking sheet.

Bake at 375 degrees for 10 to 12 minutes or until golden brown. Serve warm. You may substitute grated Parmesan cheese or bacon bits for the Cheddar cheese. *Yield: 20 twists.*

Approx Per Twist: Cal 47; Prot 1 g; Carbo 4 g; T Fat 3 g; 55% Calories from Fat; Chol 2 mg; Fiber <1 g; Sod 117 mg; Vit A 6 RE; Vit C 0 mg; Ca 8 mg; Iron <1 mg

Wars have been fought and countries discovered because of treasured spices. Marco Polo's stories of his trip to China in the late 1200s told of the spice trade in these then unknown lands and brought many Europeans in search of spices. In the fifteenth to seventeenth centuries the Spanish, English, Portuguese, and Dutch traders competed in the spice trade from the Far East. By the 1800s America was involved in the spice trade. America's first millionaires made their money in the spice trade.

Warm Winter Fruit Compote

Serve warm as a dessert topped with vanilla nonfat yogurt, for brunch over oatmeal or waffles, or as a snack. Equally good served cold.

1	(16-ounce) can pear halves or sliced peaches in light syrup	4	ounces dried apricots
4	ounces dried dates or prunes	•	Juice of ½ lemon
		½	teaspoon vanilla extract
		¼	teaspoon cinnamon

Drain the pears, reserving the syrup. Mix the pears, dates and apricots in a microwave-safe dish. Drizzle with a mixture of the lemon juice and vanilla. Sprinkle with the cinnamon. Add just enough of the reserved syrup to barely cover the fruit.

Microwave, covered, on High for 10 to 15 minutes or until the fruits are tender. You may bake in a conventional oven at 350 degrees for 45 minutes. You may substitute juice-pack fruit, fresh ripe pears and drained canned apricots if desired. *Yield: 6 servings.*

Approx Per Serving: Cal 147; Prot 1 g; Carbo 38 g; T Fat <1 g; 1% Calories from Fat; Chol 0 mg; Fiber 4 g; Sod 5 mg; Vit A 16 RE; Vit C 5 mg; Ca 19 mg; Iron 1 mg
The nutritional information includes the entire amount of the syrup.

For a quick and easy marinade, combine one acidic ingredient, one herb, and one flavoring from the following ingredients: Acidic— lemon juice, orange juice, or vinegar; Herb—tarragon, dillweed, or thyme; Flavoring—garlic, gingerroot, or soy sauce. Be creative. The combination possibilities are endless.

SPICY POACHED PEARS

2	cups cranberry juice or zinfandel	1	teaspoon vanilla extract
¼	cup frozen orange juice concentrate, or ¼ teaspoon grated orange zest	½	teaspoon grated lemon zest
		¼	teaspoon ground cloves
2	tablespoons sugar	4	ripe pears, peeled, cut into halves
2	cinnamon sticks, or ¼ teaspoon cinnamon		

Combine the cranberry juice, orange juice concentrate, sugar, cinnamon sticks, vanilla, lemon zest and cloves in a saucepan and mix well. Bring to a simmer. Simmer for 5 minutes. Add the pears. Bring to a boil; reduce heat.

Simmer, covered, for 10 to 15 minutes or just until tender, stirring occasionally. Serve the pears warm, at room temperature or chilled. Drizzle each pear half with some of the poaching liquid. You may prepare several days in advance and store, covered, in the refrigerator in the poaching liquid. *Yield: 8 servings.*

Approx Per Serving: Cal 111; Prot 1 g; Carbo 28 g; T Fat <1 g; 3% Calories from Fat; Chol 0 mg; Fiber 2 g; Sod 2 mg; Vit A 4 RE; Vit C 38 mg; Ca 14 mg; Iron <1 mg

SCALLOPED PINEAPPLE

From York River Inn in Yorktown, Virginia. Serve as a side dish with roasted meats or on a breakfast buffet.

1	(20-ounce) can juice-pack pineapple chunks	1	teaspoon lemon juice	
1	cup sugar	1/2	teaspoon vanilla extract	
1/2	cup packed brown sugar	1/2	teaspoon salt	
1/2	cup half-and-half	1/8	teaspoon nutmeg	
1/2	cup (1 stick) butter, melted	3	cups Hawaiian bread crumbs	
3	eggs, beaten			

Combine the undrained pineapple, sugar, brown sugar, half-and-half, butter, eggs, lemon juice, vanilla, salt and nutmeg in a bowl and mix gently. Fold in the bread crumbs.

Spoon the pineapple mixture into a greased 7x11-inch baking dish. Bake at 350 degrees for 45 minutes. *Yield: 8 servings.*

Approx Per Serving: Cal 392; Prot 4 g; Carbo 59 g; T Fat 16 g; 37% Calories from Fat; Chol 116 mg; Fiber 1 g; Sod 397 mg; Vit A 162 RE; Vit C 7 mg; Ca 50 mg; Iron 1 mg

For a quick and easy brunch item, sprinkle minced fresh mint over fresh pineapple chunks and drizzle with a few drops of peppermint liqueur.

ROASTED AND SUN-DRIED TOMATO SALSA

Recipe furnished by Belle Kuisine of Richmond, Virginia.

6	ripe tomatoes, cored	3	tablespoons fresh lime juice
¼	cup extra-virgin olive oil	1	garlic clove, minced
¼	cup finely chopped oil-pack sun-dried tomatoes	¼	teaspoon salt, or to taste
¼	cup chopped fresh marjoram	¼	teaspoon freshly ground pepper, or to taste

Slice the tomatoes horizontally into halves and discard the seeds. Rub the tomato halves with the olive oil. Arrange in a baking pan. Bake at 550 degrees for 15 minutes or until roasted. Cool slightly.

Chop the tomatoes into bite-size pieces. Combine the roasted tomatoes, sun-dried tomatoes, marjoram, lime juice and garlic in a bowl and mix well. Stir in the salt and pepper. Chill, covered, until serving time or for up to 3 days. You may roast the tomatoes over hot coals if desired.
Yield: 4 servings.

Approx Per Serving: Cal 177; Prot 2 g; Carbo 11 g; T Fat 15 g; 72% Calories from Fat; Chol 0 mg; Fiber 2 g; Sod 180 mg; Vit A 123 RE; Vit C 46 mg; Ca 15 mg; Iron 1 mg

CAJUN ONION MUSTARD

1	cup minced onion	1/2	teaspoon crushed
3/4	cup minced red bell		red pepper
	pepper	1	cup prepared mustard
1/4	cup sugar		

Combine the onion, bell pepper, sugar and crushed red pepper in a saucepan. Cook over medium heat until the sugar dissolves, stirring constantly. Cook for 20 minutes longer or until the liquid evaporates, stirring frequently. Let stand until cool.

Stir the mustard into the onion mixture. Spoon into a glass container with a tight-fitting lid. Store in the refrigerator. Serve as a relish or use as a sandwich spread. *Yield: 12 (2-tablespoon) servings.*

Approx Per Serving: Cal 51; Prot 1 g; Carbo 10 g; T Fat 1 g; 16% Calories from Fat; Chol 0 mg; Fiber 1 g; Sod 262 mg; Vit A 53 RE; Vit C 21 mg; Ca 30 mg; Iron 1 mg

MAKE-YOUR-OWN CURRY

1/4	cup coriander seeds	1	teaspoon ginger
1/4	cup turmeric	1	teaspoon cardamom seeds
1	(4-inch) cinnamon stick,	5	whole cloves
	broken	2	bay leaves
1	tablespoon cumin seeds		
1	teaspoon black		
	peppercorns		

Combine the coriander seeds, turmeric, cinnamon stick, cumin seeds, peppercorns, ginger, cardamom seeds, cloves and bay leaves in a shallow baking pan and mix well. Bake at 200 degrees for 25 minutes, stirring occasionally. Process the spice mixture in a blender until ground. Store in a jar with a tight-fitting lid. *Yield: 12 (1-tablespoon) servings.*

Approx Per Serving: Cal 16; Prot 1 g; Carbo 3 g; T Fat 1 g; 30% Calories from Fat; Chol 0 mg; Fiber 1 g; Sod 2 mg; Vit A 1 RE; Vit C 1 mg; Ca 21 mg; Iron 2 mg

The proportions of a classic vinaigrette are three to four parts of oil to one part lemon juice, lime juice, or vinegar, with salt and pepper to taste. A dry red wine may be substituted for the vinegar, and other herbs may be added. Garlic cloves and herbs should be removed from the vinaigrette after twenty-four hours.

Use rubs on tender cuts of meat to add flavor. To apply the rub, cover the outside surface of the beef with the seasoning blend prior to cooking or grilling. The flavor is enhanced the longer the standing time.

LEMON ROSEMARY RUB

1½ teaspoons grated lemon zest

1 teaspoon rosemary leaves, crushed

¼ teaspoon salt

¼ teaspoon thyme leaves

¼ teaspoon coarsely ground pepper

2 large garlic cloves, minced

Combine the lemon zest, rosemary, salt, thyme, pepper and garlic in a bowl and mix well. Store in an airtight container. Shake before using.
Yield: 4 teaspoons (Enough to season 2 pounds of beef).

Approx Per Recipe: Cal 23; Prot 1 g; Carbo 5 g; T Fat <1 g; 11% Calories from Fat; Chol 0 mg; Fiber 2 g; Sod 584 mg; Vit A 7 RE; Vit C 6 mg; Ca 50 mg; Iron 1 mg

SPICY SEASONING RUB

3 tablespoons chili powder

2 teaspoons coriander

2 teaspoons cumin

1½ teaspoons garlic powder

¾ teaspoon oregano leaves

½ teaspoon ground red pepper

Combine the chili powder, coriander, cumin, garlic powder, oregano and red pepper in a bowl and mix well. Store in an airtight container. Shake before using. *Yield: 5¼ tablespoons (Enough to season 2 pounds of beef).*

Approx Per Recipe: Cal 109; Prot 5 g; Carbo 19 g; T Fat 5 g; 32% Calories from Fat; Chol 0 mg; Fiber 9 g; Sod 238 mg; Vit A 835 RE; Vit C 23 mg; Ca 119 mg; Iron 7 mg

LEMONY ORIENTAL MARINADE

- ¼ cup fresh lemon juice
- 3 tablespoons chopped green onions
- 1½ tablespoons reduced-sodium soy sauce
- 1½ tablespoons vegetable oil
- ¾ teaspoon grated gingerroot
- ¼ teaspoon crushed red pepper pods

Combine the lemon juice, green onions, soy sauce, oil, gingerroot and red pepper in a bowl and mix well. Use as a marinade for beef, poultry and seafood. *Yield: ½ cup.*

Approx Per Recipe: Cal 224; Prot 3 g; Carbo 10 g; T Fat 21 g; 78% Calories from Fat; Chol 0 mg; Fiber 1 g; Sod 762 mg; Vit A 9 RE; Vit C 32 mg; Ca 23 mg; Iron <1 mg

RED WINE MARINADE

- ⅓ cup red wine vinegar
- 2 tablespoons vegetable oil
- 1 tablespoon Dijon mustard
- 2 garlic cloves, minced
- ¾ teaspoon Italian seasoning
- ¼ teaspoon coarsely ground pepper

Combine the wine vinegar, oil, Dijon mustard, garlic, Italian seasoning and pepper in a bowl and mix well. Use as a marinade for beef, poultry or seafood. *Yield: ½ cup.*

Approx Per Recipe: Cal 297; Prot 1 g; Carbo 4 g; T Fat 29 g; 92% Calories from Fat; Chol 0 mg; Fiber <1 g; Sod 385 mg; Vit A <1 RE; Vit C 2 mg; Ca 38 mg; Iron 1 mg

Allow approximately ¼ to ½ cup marinade for each one to two pounds of beef. Turn the beef occasionally during the marinating process so that all sides are equally exposed to the marinade. For flavor only, marinate for fifteen minutes or up to two hours in the refrigerator. For tenderizing, marinate in the refrigerator for six hours or longer. The remaining marinade may be brushed on the beef during the grilling process or used as a sauce, provided it is brought to a rolling boil for at least one minute prior to serving.

How to Read a Food Label

Macaroni & Cheese

Nutrition Facts

Start Here ➡

Serving Size 1 cup (228g)
Servings Per Container 2

Amount Per Serving

Calories 250   Calories from Fat 110

	% Daily Value*
Total Fat 12g	**18%**
Saturated Fat 3g	**15%**
Cholesterol 30mg	**10%**
Sodium 470mg	**20%**
Total Carbohydrate 31g	**10%**
Dietary Fiber 0g	**0%**
Sugars 5g	
Protein 5g	
Vitamin A	4%
Vitamin C	2%
Calcium	20%
Iron	4%

Limit these Nutrients

Get Enough of these Nutrients

Quick Guide to %DV

5% or less is Low;

20% or more is High

*Percent Daily Values are based on a 2,000 calorie diet. Your Daily Values may be higher or lower depending on your calorie needs:

	Calories:	2,000	2,500
Total Fat	Less than	65g	80g
Sat Fat	Less than	20g	25g
Cholesterol	Less than	300mg	300mg
Sodium	Less than	2,400mg	2,400mg
Total Carbohydrate		300g	375g
Dietary Fiber		25g	30g

Footnote

Understanding Food Labels

The food label can be found on food packages in your supermarket. Reading the label tells more about the food and what you are purchasing. What you see on the food label is required by the government.

- The SERVING SIZE tells the size or portion referred to in the nutrition facts. Read the labels carefully because some serving sizes state "...⅓ of the individually wrapped muffin."
- CALORIES and CALORIES FROM FAT: A recommendation is that "Only 30% of your total calories for the day should come from fat."
- TOTAL FAT: Five grams of fat equals a teaspoon of margarine or oil or one small strip of bacon.
- SATURATED FAT A recommendation is no more than 10% of the total fat calories from saturated fat.
- CHOLESTEROL intake should be below 300 milligrams per day. The liver makes cholesterol, and a higher-fat diet will stimulate this production.
- SODIUM: Registered Dietitians recommend staying between 4000 to 5000 milligrams per day. Convenience items and canned items are usually very high.
- TOTAL CARBOHYDRATE: Fifteen grams is one carbohydrate exchange, or one slice of bread. Registered Dietitians recommend at least 11 to 12 servings of carbohydrates a day. Read the labels to figure how many 15-gram units are in an item.
- FIBER: The recommended intake per day is 20 to 30 grams.
- SUGAR: Read the label to distinguish natural sugar from added sugar.
- TOTAL PROTEIN: The average adult needs about 6 ounces of protein per day. Vegetarians must be sure to include complementary proteins such as beans and rice to match the biological value of meat. Their bonus is a diet rich in fiber and low in fat.
- VITAMINS and MINERALS: Only the vitamins A and C, and the minerals calcium and iron, are on the food labels, because they are the nutrients in which US diets are most often deficient.
- DAILY VALUES for fat and carbohydrate are based on a 2000-calorie diet. DAILY VALUES for vitamins and minerals are based on adult values.

FOOD GUIDE PYRAMID

A Guide to Daily Food Choices

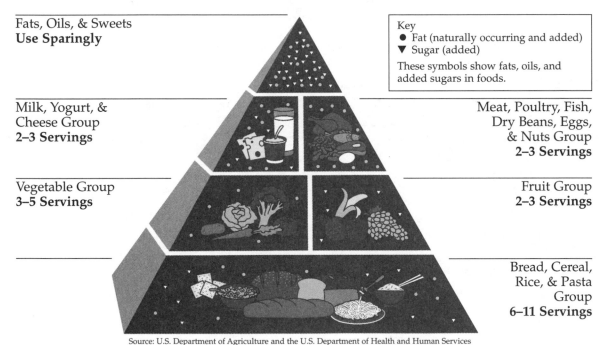

Fats, Oils, & Sweets
Use Sparingly

Key
● Fat (naturally occurring and added)
▼ Sugar (added)

These symbols show fats, oils, and added sugars in foods.

Milk, Yogurt, &
Cheese Group
2–3 Servings

Meat, Poultry, Fish,
Dry Beans, Eggs,
& Nuts Group
2–3 Servings

Vegetable Group
3–5 Servings

Fruit Group
2–3 Servings

Bread, Cereal,
Rice, & Pasta
Group
6–11 Servings

Source: U.S. Department of Agriculture and the U.S. Department of Health and Human Services

What Counts as a Serving?

Bread, Cereal, Rice, and Pasta
1 slice bread
1 ounce ready-to-eat cereal
½ cup cooked cereal, rice, or pasta

Fruit
1 medium apple, banana, or orange
½ cup canned, cooked chopped fruit
¾ cup fruit juice

Vegetables
1 cup raw leafy vegetables
½ cup other vegetables, cooked
¾ cup vegetable juice

Milk, Yogurt, and Cheese
1 cup milk or yogurt
1½ ounces natural cheese
2 ounces process cheese

Meat, Poultry, Fish, Dry Beans, Eggs, and Nuts
2 to 3 ounces cooked lean meat, poultry, or fish
½ cup cooked dry beans, 1 egg, or 2 tablespoons
     peanut butter count as 1 ounce lean meat

MEASUREMENT EQUIVALENTS

3 teaspoons . . . . 1 tablespoon

2 tablespoons . . . . ⅛ cup

4 tablespoons . . . . ¼ cup

5 tablespoons + 1 teaspoon . . . . ⅓ cup

8 tablespoons . . . . ½ cup

12 tablespoons . . . . ¾ cup

16 tablespoons . . . . 1 cup

32 tablespoons . . . . 2 cups

64 tablespoons . . . . 1 quart

96 tablespoons . . . . 1½ quarts

1 ounce . . . . 2 tablespoons fat or liquid

4 ounces . . . . ½ cup

8 ounces . . . . 1 cup

16 ounces . . . . 1 pound

⅝ cup . . . . ½ cup + 2 tablespoons = 10 tablespoons

⅞ cup . . . . ¾ cup + 2 tablespoons = 14 tablespoons

2 cups . . . . 1 pint

2 pints . . . . 1 quart

1 quart . . . . 4 cups

4 quarts . . . . 1 gallon

Nutritional Profile Guidelines

The editors have attempted to present these family recipes in a format that allows approximate nutritional values to be computed. Persons with dietary or health problems or whose diets require close monitoring should not rely solely on the nutritional information provided. They should consult their physician or a registered dietitian for specific information.

Abbreviations for Nutritional Profile

Cal — Calories	T Fat — Total Fat	Sod — Sodium
Prot — Protein	Chol — Cholesterol	g — grams
Carbo — Carbohydrates	Fiber — Dietary Fiber	mg — milligrams

Nutritional information for these recipes is computed from information derived from many sources, including materials supplied by the United States Department of Agriculture, computer databanks, and journals in which the information is assumed to be in the public domain. However, many specialty items, new products, and processed food may not be available from these sources or may vary from the average values used in these profiles. More information on new and/or specific products may be obtained by reading the nutrient labels. Unless otherwise specified, the nutritional profile of these recipes is based on all measurements being level.

- Artificial sweeteners vary in use and strength and should be used to taste, using the recipe ingredients as a guideline. Sweeteners using aspartame (NutraSweet and Equal) should not be used as a sweetener in recipes involving prolonged heating, which reduces the sweet taste. For further information on the use of these sweeteners, refer to the package.
- Alcoholic ingredients have been analyzed for the basic information. Cooking causes the evaporation of alcohol, which decreases alcoholic and caloric content.
- Buttermilk, sour cream, and yogurt are the types available commercially.
- Canned beans and vegetables have been analyzed with the canning liquid. Rinsing and draining canned products will lower the sodium content.
- Chicken, cooked for boning and chopping, has been roasted; this cooking method yields the lowest caloric values.
- Eggs are all large. To avoid raw eggs that may carry salmonella, as in eggnog or 6-week muffin batter, use an equivalent amount of commercial egg substitute.
- Flour is unsifted all-purpose flour.
- Garnishes, serving suggestions, and other optional information and variations are not included in the profile.
- Margarine and butter are regular, not whipped or presoftened.
- Oil is any type of vegetable cooking oil. Shortening is hydrogenated vegetable shortening.
- Salt and other ingredients to taste as noted in the ingredients have not been included in the nutritional profile.
- If a choice of ingredients has been given, the profile reflects the first option. If a choice of amounts has been given, the profile reflects the greater amount.

Contributors & Testers

Linda Aills • Lucy Lisenby Andrews • Cathy Angotti

Cyndi Atterbury • Linda Barnes • Erna Mae Behrend • Belle Kuisine

Jane Blosser • Kris Bonham • Jane Bordwine • Sandy Bosworth

Patricia B. Brevard • Audrey Burt • Debi and Chip Burt • Karren Case

Lynne Cauble • Carol Clark • Christine Clay • Ellen Coale

Lynn Cookson-Earle • L. Clare Costello • Donna Crotts • Shirley Dana

Jackie Darling • Linda Davis • Diana Deputy • Lynn Dorman

Pam Dowker • Anne Newton Dumper • Dana L. Egan • Shirley Eley

Kim Ellis • Mindy Facenda • Sarah Flash • Linda Foster • Lu Foster

Lucy Garman • Patricia Garrett • Jean Jessee Gilmer • Janet Gloeckner

Shayna Gonsky • Caroline Hackley • Karen Hansrote • Mary Harshfield

Lynne Henshaw • Ann Hertzler • Pamela Hoffstetter • Myrtle Hogbin

Iva Mary Hopkins • Fran Johnson • Pat Johnson • Carol E. Jones

Jennifer Jordan • Beverly Kates • Christofer Kelly • Carol King

Lynne Latino • Yvonne W. Lavender • Valerie H. Lewis

Chris Loudon • Brenda Lucas • Janice MacLeod • Don Mankie

George Marrah • Anita McAllister • Penny E. McConnell

Julie Mercado • Judy Mitnick • Linda Mlot • Mildred Moore

Peggy Morgan • Barbara Blauvelt Morlang • Linda Morrison

Connie Nyberg • Jenny Okon • Nancy Ortiz • Gale Pearson

Chris Reeb • Krystal Register • Sandra Rhodes • Angela Richter

Pam Ritchson • Jean Robbins • Mary Jo Sawyer • Karen Schultz

Kim Seador • Nanette Showalter • Cindy Shufflebarger

Suzi Silverstein • Rita Smith • Loretta M. Tom • Jennifer Tu

Isabel Vartanian • Virgina Beef Cattlemen's Association

Virginia Department of Agriculture and Consumer Services

Ellen Wade • Tammy Wagner • Kathleen Walters

Barbara Watts • Chris Zirpoli

BIBLIOGRAPHY

Acton, Eliza. *Modern Cookery.* Revised by Mrs. S. J. Hale. Philadelphia: John E. Potter and Co., 1885.

Bennion, M. "Food Preparation in Colonial America," *Journal of the American Dietetic Association*, Vol. 69:16. Chicago: 1976.

Beroizheimer, Ruth. *The American Woman's Cook Book.* Chicago: Consolidated Book Publishers, Inc., 1943.

Better Homes and Gardens Heritage Cook Book, Better Homes and Gardens. Des Moines, Iowa: Meredith Corp., 1975.

Bullock, Helen. *The Williamsburg Art of Cookery.* Richmond: Colonial Williamsburg, Inc., Dec. 1938.

The Butterick Book of Recipes and Household Helps. New York: The Butterick Publishing Company, 1927.

Carlton, Jan. *More Richmond Receipts—past and present.* Norfolk: J. & B. Editions, 1990.

Crump, Nancy Carter. *Hearthside Cooking.* McLean, Va.: EPM Publications, Inc., 1986.

Dabney, Joseph E. *Smokehouse Ham, Spoonbread, & Scuppernong Wine— The Folklore and Art of Southern Appalachian Cooking.* Nashville, Tenn.: Cumberland House, 1998.

Egerton, John. "Roots of Southern Food," *Southern Living, 1990 Annual Recipes.* Birmingham: Oxmoor House, 1990.

Egerton, John. *Southern Food.* Chapel Hill, N.C.: The University of North Carolina Press, 1993.

Eighteenth Century Recipes. Philadelphia: U.S. Dept. of Labor, National Park Service, U.S. Dept. of Interior. Independence National Historical Park.

Favorite Recipes of Jefferson's Country. Members of Grace Church, Cismont, Va. Charlottesville, Va.: The Wayside Press, 1971.

Haskell, Mrs. E. F. Edited by R. L. Shep. *Civil War Cooking: The Housekeepers Encyclopedia.* Mendocino, Calif.: R. L. Shep, 1992.

Hertzler, Ann A., Ph.D., R.D. "Recipes and Nutrition Education," *Journal of the American Dietetic Association,* Vol. 83, No. 4, Chicago: 1983.

Horry, Harriott Pinckney. *A Colonial Plantation Cookbook: The Receipt Book of Harriott Pinckney Horry, 1770.* Edited with an Introduction by Richard J. Hooker. Columbia, S.C.: University of South Carolina Press, 1984.

BIBLIOGRAPHY

Interesting Facts About Virginia Foods, 1607–1700. Compiled and Published by the Community Nutrition Section of the Virginia Dietetic Association and the Dairy Council of Richmond, 1957.

Ireland, Lynne. *The Compiled Cookbook as Foodways Autobiography.* Lanham, Md.: Rowman & Lituefield Publishers, Inc., 1998.

Jefferson and Wine. Vol. III, Nos. 1 & 2. Edited by R. de Treville Lawrence, Sr. The Plains, Va.: Vinifera Wine Growers Assoc., 1976.

Kander, Mrs. Simon. *The Settlement Cook Book—The Way to a Man's Heart.* Milwaukee: The Settlement Cook Book Co., 1901.

Kimball, Marie. *Thomas Jefferson's Cook Book.* Charlottesville, Va.: University Press of Virginia, 1976.

Kornblueh, M. and H. C. Parke. *Survey of the Use of Written Recipes.* Vol. 47:113–115. Chicago: Journal of the American Dietetic Association, Aug. 1965.

Leahy, Richard G. *A History of Virginia Wine: A Summary.* Richmond, Va.: Virginia Wine Country, 1998.

The Monticello Cook Book. 3rd Edition, Revised. Richmond, Va.: The Dietz Press, Inc., 1950.

Moore, Helen. "All The Presidents' Menus," the *Charlotte Observer,* Charlotte, N.C.: July 1, 1976.

Randolph, Mary. *The Virginia House-wife, 1824.* With Historical Notes and Commentaries by Karen Hess. Columbia, S.C.: University of South Carolina Press, 1984.

Recipes from Old Virginia. Compiled by The Virginia Federation of Home Demonstration Clubs. Richmond, Va.: The Dietz Press, Inc., 1964.

Redman, D., R. Jenkins, B. Mize, and William Mann, Jr. *Four Great Southern Cooks.* Atlanta: DuBose Publishing, 1980.

Robbins, Jean, Ph.D. *Food and People.* Publication 503. Blacksburg, Va.: VPI and SU, Extension Division, Oct. 1973.

Rusch, Hermann G. and Martina Neely. *The Hermann Rusch Greenbrier Cookbook.* Chicago: Contemporary Books, Inc., 1975.

Sage Advice. The Herb Society of Southwestern Virginia, Roanoke, Va. Savannah, Tenn.: Fund Co. Publishers, Inc., 1989.

The Smithfield Cookbook. The Junior Woman's Club of Smithfield, Smithfield, Va. Edited by Caroline D. Hurt and Joan H. Powell. Hampton, Va.: Multi-Print, 1978.

BIBLIOGRAPHY

Southern Living: 1990 Annual Recipes. Birmingham: Oxmoor House, Inc., 1990.

Southern Sideboards. Compiled by Junior League of Jackson, Miss. Memphis: S. C. Toof & Co., 1979.

Spencer, Maryellen, Ph.D. *Food in Seventeenth-Century Tidewater Virginia: A Method for Studying Historical Cuisines.* Dissertation, VPI and SU, Blacksburg, Va., 1982.

Tastefully Yours—Virginia. Compiled by Libby Lowance. Virginia State Chamber of Commerce, Richmond, Va. Richmond, Va.: The Williams Printing Co., 1976.

Todhunter, Neige, Ph.D. "Seven Centuries of Cookbooks—Treasures and Pleasures," *Nutrition Today.* Baltimore: Williams and Wilkins, Jan./Feb. 1992.

Torisky, D. M., R. F. Foucor-Szocki, and J. B. Walker. *Quantity Feeding During the American Civil War.* New York, N.Y.: The Haworth Press, Inc., 1998.

Tyler, Payne B. *The Virginia Presidential Homes Cookbook.* Charles City, Va.: Historic Sherwood Forest Corp., 1995.

Vaughn, Kate Brew. *Culinary Echos From Dixie.* Cincinnati: The McDonald Press Publishers, 1914.

Virginia Cookery—Past and Present. Franconia, Va.: The Woman's Auxiliary of Olivet Episcopal Church, 1957.

Virginia Seasons—New Recipes from the Old Dominion. Junior League of Richmond. Richmond: Colonial Printing and Stationery Co., Inc., 1984.

Wallace, Lily Haxworth. *The Rumford Complete Cook Book.* Rumford Chemical Works, Providence, R.I. Cambridge, Mass.: The University Press, 1908.

The Williamsburg Cookbook. Published by The Colonial Williamsburg Foundation, Williamsburg, Va., 1971.

Ziemann, Hugo and Mrs. F. L. Gillette. *The White House Cook Book.* New York: The Saalfield Publishing Co., 1906.

INDEX

INDEX

INDEX

INDEX

INDEX

INDEX

A History of Good Taste

The Virginia Dietetic Association Cookbook

Please send me _____ copies of *Vintage Virginia* at $19.95* per book $ _____

Virginia and New York residents add sales tax $ _____

Shipping / handling at $5.00 for first book plus $.50 for each additional book $ _____

Total $ _____

_____
Name

_____
Street Address

_____
City   State   Zip

_____
Telephone

Method of Payment: [   ] VISA   [   ] MasterCard

[   ] Check enclosed payable to Pocahontas Press

_____
Account Number   Expiration Date

_____
Cardholder Name

_____
Signature

Mail orders to:

Pocahontas Press • PO Drawer F • Blacksburg, Virginia 24063

1-800-446-0467 • Pocahontas.Press@vt.edu

*For orders of 6 or more books, please contact Pocahontas Press for discount information.

Photocopies will be accepted.

The Virginia Dietetic Association Cookbook